The Relationship Skills Workbook

THE RELATIONSHIP SKILLS WORKBOOK

A Do-It-Yourself Guide to a Thriving Relationship

JULIA B. COLWELL, PhD

SOUNDS TRUE
BOULDER, COLORADO

Sounds True
Boulder, CO 80306

Cover design by Rachael Murray
Book design by Beth Skelley

Printed in the United States of America

Library of Congress Cataloging-in-Publication Data
Colwell, Julia B.
  The relationship skills workbook : a do-it-yourself guide to
a thriving relationship / Julia B. Colwell, PhD.
      pages cm
  Includes bibliographical references.
  ISBN 978-1-62203-227-3
  1. Interpersonal relations. 2. Social psychology. I. Title.
  HM1106.C646 2014
  302—dc23
                                        2014010439

Ebook ISBN 978-1-62203-387-4

10 9 8 7 6 5 4 3 2 1

To Katie and Gay Hendricks. What I've learned from you has transformed every moment of my life.

And still, after all this time, the Sun has never said to the Earth,
"You owe me."
Look what happens with love like that.
It lights up the sky.

RUMI

CONTENTS

Acknowledgments . . . xi

Introduction . . . xiii

PART ONE **The Possibility: Real Self, True Connection**

CHAPTER 1 Would You Rather Be Right or Be Happy? . . . 3

CHAPTER 2 Speaking the Unarguable Truth . . . 13

PART TWO **Listening to Your Body**

CHAPTER 3 Understanding the Five Basic Emotions . . . 29

CHAPTER 4 Feeling Too Good . . . 41

CHAPTER 5 Emotions: Energy in Motion . . . 45

CHAPTER 6 The How-To's of Moving Emotions . . . 51

CHAPTER 7 Bringing It Back into Relationship . . . 59

CHAPTER 8 Advanced Tips for Emotional Mastery . . . 63

CHAPTER 9 Emotional Flow: Blocks and Unblocking . . . 73

CHAPTER 10 Relationship as Emotional Healer . . . 87

PART THREE **The Route to True Power**

CHAPTER 11 Taking Healthy Responsibility . . . 95

CHAPTER 12 Three Toxic Habits to Break . . . 103

CHAPTER 13 Empowerment through Integrity . . . 111

CHAPTER 14   Making Great and Successful Agreements . . . 117

CHAPTER 15   From Power Struggle to Empowerment . . . 131

CHAPTER 16   Judgment and Defense . . . 141

CHAPTER 17   The Triangle: Getting Stuck
             in Power Struggle . . . 147

PART FOUR   **Living the Biggest Relationship
            You Can Imagine**

CHAPTER 18   A Dream Come True . . . 159

CHAPTER 19   Appreciations . . . 163

CHAPTER 20   Moving between Expansiveness
             and Contraction . . . 169

CHAPTER 21   Creativity and Play . . . 171

CHAPTER 22   Choosing Aliveness . . . 175

CHAPTER 23   Choosing Love . . . 177

CHAPTER 24   Learning to Love Yourself . . . 179

EPILOGUE   Traveling the Path to a
            Magical Relationship . . . 183

APPENDIX 1   Quick Guide to Making a Choice . . . 185

APPENDIX 2   Sample Answers to Arguable/Unarguable
             Truth Exercise . . . 187

APPENDIX 3   The Inner Map . . . 189

             Notes . . . 195

             Resources . . . 197

             About the Author . . . 201

Tool Kit Exercises

Try It Out . . . 9

Committing to Happiness . . . 11

Describe Your Sensations . . . 15

Moving from the Arguable to the Unarguable
   (Sensations and Emotions) . . . 18

Calibrating Your Yes and Your No . . . 21

Unearthing What You Really Want and Don't Want . . . 21

Tracking and Translating the Arguable . . . 25

Shifting a Conflict . . . 26

From Sensations to Emotions . . . 38

Translating Your Emotions . . . 39

Upper Limits and Rest . . . 43

Upper Limit Detection . . . 43

Moving Emotions Process . . . 57

Openhearted Listening Checklist . . . 61

Moving through Emotions Together . . . 62

Time-Out Worksheet . . . 78

Labeling Your Drifts . . . 80

Creating a Shift Repertoire . . . 85

Committing to Shifting . . . 85

Conscious Complaining . . . 86

Committing to Blaming or to Taking Responsibility . . . 106

Moving from Blame to Power . . . 107

Blame and Complaint Log . . . 108

Blame and Complaint Diet . . . 108

How Do I Know I'm Taking 100 Percent Responsibility? . . . 109

What Does Feeling Powerful Actually Feel Like? . . . 112

Dialing Yourself into Your Life . . . 116

Integrity Inventory . . . 116

Getting to the Bottom Line . . . 127

Making a Great and Successful Agreement . . . 128

How I Created This/What I'll Do Differently . . . 136

How I Try to Control Others . . . 140

Practicing Moving Out of Judgment . . . 142

Practicing Moving Out of Defensiveness . . . 143

Power Inventory . . . 145

Becoming Aware of the Triangle . . . 150

The World and the Triangle . . . 150

Getting Out of the Triangle . . . 152

Knowing When You're in the Triangle . . . 154

Your Relationship Well-Being Bank Account . . . 155

Intending the Relationship You Really Want . . . 160

Lighting the Appreciation Flame . . . 165

Appreciating Your Partner . . . 166

Appreciating Yourself . . . 167

Generating and Receiving Appreciations . . . 168

Tracking Your Contraction and Expansion . . . 170

Moving from Contraction to Expansion . . . 170

Follow Your Impulses . . . 173

Follow Your Impulses Together . . . 173

How Can We Have More Fun? . . . 174

Choosing Aliveness . . . 176

Creating Connection . . . 177

Dates and Mystery Dates . . . 178

Date Plan . . . 178

Learning to Love Yourself . . . 180

Writing Love Letters . . . 181

ACKNOWLEDGMENTS

As I look back through my journey to understanding what I do about relationships, I see a long line of wise teachers. I communed with many of those through their written words, taking in their ideas as I was soaking up their expanded energy. Meanwhile, my heart is full as I remember the therapists, guides, and teachers with whom I had the good fortune to physically share time and space. I am awed at being on the planet at the same time as people of this depth, intellect, and magnificence of soul.

I am forever grateful to my beloved mentors and teachers, Kathlyn and Gay Hendricks, for their wisdom, mastery, and love in educating me about conscious relationships. This workbook is based heavily on what I have embodied from their transformational teachings. You'll see where I've adapted and included exercises of theirs in this workbook that I've found to be particularly powerful. There are many people writing today about the need to expand our consciousness; Gay and Katie have provided a crucial missing piece, creating revolutionary tools that provide the *how* behind such a monumental task.

I would also like to thank my other guides: Gail Kali, Ethel Greene, Barbara Green, Lin Harden, Ellen Maslow, and Barbara Griek for their knowledge and direction. I am grateful to my wonderful editor from Sounds True, Haven Iverson; to Tami Simon, for her vision of there being a place in the world for this sort of relationship book; and to the welcoming and high-powered Sounds True family. Finally, I offer deep gratitude and appreciation to my supportive friends and family, to the hundreds of clients who allowed me to share their journeys through their deepest sorrows to their greatest triumphs, and to all of the co-creators, participants, and colleagues of the Boulder Center for Conscious Community.

Now, I want to acknowledge my greatest teacher of all, my spouse Kathryn Kucsan. Kath has so many qualities that have created space for my deepest learning: her playfulness, whimsy, and ability to laugh at the height of our "serious" conversations; her many-dimensioned intellect and ability to ask the biggest questions; her connection to invisible and other non-human worlds; her willingness to face into the deepest truths, no matter how painful; and her huge heart. As I write, I feel overwhelmed by the power of her inner universe, and feel grateful to have inhabited it with her. It is her extraordinary grit and determination, though, that I see as pivotal in keeping us on the path when the lessons were the hardest and I most wanted to flee. During our darkest times, she carried the torch of the possibilities that were over on the other side of the mountain.

Kath also knew from the very beginning that "we had work to do together." She urged me to write our story down so that others could benefit from what we had learned. The first version of this workbook, called *Choosing Love: Pathways to Conscious Relationship,* was our venture into sharing our experiences and most valuable lessons. You'll hear the echo of Kath's strong, sweet voice and loving, open heart in the pages of *The Relationship Skills Workbook.* I know that it is her hope, as it is mine, that you will benefit from what we've learned together. As we've traveled through times of bliss, times of challenge, and ultimately, always, deeper reconnection, we have discovered a place of co-creativity and expansion, of daily joy and connection, and a level of openness where anything and everything is possible.

INTRODUCTION

I was in my early thirties when I finished my PhD in clinical psychology. In the weeks before graduation, I began a relationship. Since I'd been to graduate school, I imagined I had an advantage in sorting through the ins-and-outs of intimacy. But with all of the knowledge I'd learned in those five years of school, I was a rank beginner in understanding how to move through the power struggles I was creating. That's how I got to the brink of ending one more relationship on a fateful day, sitting on the floor across from my partner.

As a newly minted psychologist, I put my time in at the local mental health center while I started my private practice. By this time, I'd done quite a bit of personal therapy, which I continued as I viewed myself as an anxiously depressed person who occasionally stumbled on good days. I relied on my mind to make sense of my inner world, not understanding that I was putting the fox in charge of the chickens. And I, frankly, had no idea if I'd be able to create a relationship that I'd want to stay in.

I felt nervous seeing clients, and I relied on my excellent education in talking to people about what ailed them. Along the way, some couples came to me. I found myself falling back on one of the only couples therapy techniques I was aware of: reflective listening. I patiently taught each person to paraphrase the other, with the extra words of thoughtfulness, "What I heard you say is . . ." and "Did I hear you correctly?"

I did notice the small problem of not being able to actually use these skills myself. When I got angry, the last thing I wanted to do was paraphrase. I was reactive. I wanted to lash out, be right, get my point across. I figured that I just had to get better at it, that I'd learn that "paraphrasing thing" at some point in time. The couples I was seeing sat with me, dutifully parroting the words I said. When they came back and reported that they weren't able to listen, let alone reflect, we all chalked it up to them needing more time to practice.

During this time of lukewarm success, I stumbled on a book called *Conscious Loving* by some authors I'd never heard of, Gay and Kathlyn Hendricks. I was drawn to the subtitle: *A Way to Be Fully Together without Giving Up Yourself.* I had devoted my time in graduate school studying related ground, that is, the dynamics of merging and disengagement in couples, so I decided that these Hendricks people must be kindred spirits. I read the book with mild interest and started trying out some of the tools with couples, and was intrigued by how they seemed to actually be using them. I brought the book home, and my partner (a musician who must have been weary of the ways I was trying to "improve" her and us) actually read it. Weeks later, we were in one of those arguments that had become ever-too-common, and way too familiar in my sense of frustration, defensiveness, and ultimately, helplessness to shift. I sat on the floor, leaning against the wall, my arms tightly crossed in front of me. I glared at my partner, my jaw clenched. We had been at this for a while, and now were at a familiar stalemate.

I have no idea what we were fighting about. But I do know what I was fighting for—my voice, my place, my legitimacy. I wasn't willing to back down. I knew the price of losing the battle, so I kept at it. Maybe I gave up some ground here and there, but I would recapture it with my next snide comment or attack of logic.

As we sat there in silence, I felt a familiar doom. I had been through this before in previous relationships: the shutting down that led to the end. I started calculating: I was thirty-five years old and had been in this relationship for four years. We probably had another year to eke out before we called it quits. If I lived until seventy-five and every relationship lasted five years, how many more relationships would I have before I died?

My partner interrupted my thoughts. "You told me to read this book. Here it is. Let's try it."

I rolled my eyes and pulled in my body even more. Clearly, she was desperate.

"Here's this list of questions.[1] The first one says, 'What are you feeling?'"

What a stupid question. "Mad, of course."

She pushed on.

"What do you want?"

"I want this to be over!" I left my meaning vague, knowing she wouldn't miss my veiled threat about leaving.

"How is the past coloring your present?"

OK, that was familiar ground. I was the well-educated therapist who had done her work about old patterns.

"It isn't. This is about now. You won't listen to me." I felt resigned satisfaction, knowing that this wasn't going to work either.

"What are you getting out of staying stuck?"

What? Now this was a brand-new thought. I was getting something out of staying stuck? My head rose, and I felt a bit of expansion in my chest. I felt curiosity move through my body, lightening my cells as if the sun had just streamed through the window.

I don't remember how the rest of the conversation went or how we solved the issue. The real solution came in my body opening up. The palpable shift in my thinking and in my body from that moment is forever stamped in my consciousness as what mattered. I knew that I had experienced something more powerful than any better argument or more thought-out debate strategy had given me before. I had glimpsed my own unconscious pattern, the one lodged in my body. While I remember the discomfort of seeing what I was doing to keep the struggle going, the empowerment of discovering how I was creating the stuckness felt like walking through the door into a rocket ship. My body tingled as I sat in front of a whole new set of controls.

I felt better. My body relaxed. I could actually see my partner more clearly. Maybe she didn't hate me. Maybe I didn't have to see her as the enemy. Maybe there was a different way. I wanted desperately to know what that was.

I grew up couched in the norms of the late fifties and into the sixties. Siblings fought, kids slugged each other, and parents controlled their broods through criticism and threats. I knew my place, even when I had to jockey for it. Meanwhile, I felt proud of having learned to defend myself verbally and physically.

This was my relationship toolkit that I took from my childhood—which was pretty much all I had to go on for my adult relationships:

> » Be right! (And for sure, don't be wrong.)
> » Be ready to fight off other people's attempts to control me.
> » Solve problems by:
>   - Trying to fix them by figuring them out.
>   - Figuring out problems means figuring out who is to blame.
>   - Get the one who is to blame to change.
>   - When that doesn't work, try to compromise.
>   - When *that* doesn't work, fight (wheedle, whine, collapse, overpower, argue, attack).
>   - Stop fighting by withdrawing and distancing.
>   - Endure, knowing that this is as good as it gets.

Over the decades since the fateful day that I discovered a whole new list of ways through conflict and disagreement, I have dedicated myself to learning and experimenting and teaching and learning some more about the sometimes mysterious, often complicated world of relationships. I have tested everything in *The Relationship Skills Workbook* in my own relationship, while fine-tuning all of these skills through counseling and teaching hundreds of couples and individuals over thousands of hours. I am thrilled to be able to offer what I believe to be a set of tools that are on the cutting edge of human evolution and human relationship. And because of my own steep learning curve with these tools, I am optimistic that just about anyone can embody them.

Is This Book for You?

You might be wondering if this workbook will work for you. If you're a man, you might ask if a woman's perspective would be helpful; if you're heterosexual, you might wonder if a woman who has spent decades intimate with another woman has anything relevant to teach you.

My perspective on relationships is that we're all just learning. Having worked with just about every combination of people in relationships—straight, gay, not-to-be-identified, monogamous, polyamorous, parent-child, co-workers, community members, little kids to elderly—I've learned that we're just not that different from one another. (You'll notice that I switch back and forth in my pronoun use throughout the book, as I want to convey that I'm talking about anyone throughout.) Meanwhile, my own fascination with relationships comes from how challenged I've felt by them. Everything I've watched in others—the giddiness of new love and the boredom of settling in, the heartbreak of betrayal and the guilt of falling in love with someone else, the heat of reactivity and the miracle of rediscovering intimacy—has been my experience as well.

The skills in this workbook can be applied to any relationship. They might seem to be most relevant to your intimate partnership, but you'll find that they are equally effective in working through conflict, power struggle, and stuckness with your co-workers, your parents and siblings, your children, and your friends. In fact, you'll find that you can use them for the most important relationship of all: the one you have with yourself. Relationship truly is our best teacher, if we can step back, take a breath, and find what it is we most need to learn. While being about the most challenging puzzle you might ever try to solve, sticking with the challenge offers huge payoffs. What triggers us are issues from the past that are waiting to be cleared up—and there is nothing like relationship to provide an endless stream of triggers. Letting your relationships teach you what you most need to learn will allow you to be transformed from the inside out.

We may think we're from different planets (Mars and Venus come to mind) or that those who identify from another part of the gender or sexual orientation or the age, ethnic, religious, or class spectrum would never be able to see life from our perspective. But our similarities heavily outweigh our differences. We all have the same brain that can get triggered in the same frustratingly common way. We all want to be seen, known, understood, and accepted for who we really are. As pack animals, we humans are nourished by connection. As individuals looking for meaning and fulfillment, we aren't willing to give up our selves. Finding a way to be deeply connected while expressing who we truly are is what this book is all about.

Using This Workbook

My passion in writing this workbook is that I know first-hand—through my own life, through watching hundreds of my clients struggle—the great suffering that people go through because they don't have the basic tools for having even a decent relationship. And I know that most people could go way beyond just "decent" to truly magnificent relationships if they knew a few key concepts and skills. It is my belief and my experience that the intense connection, the passion, and the flow of life energy that are the juice of new relationships can be created and cultivated no matter how long two people have been involved.

So I invite you to dive into this workbook. Write in it, underline, highlight, and draw pictures in the margins. Get a separate journal to carry around with you to do the exercises that I'll ask you to do. As you try things out, give yourself plenty of space to fail, to not get it, and to try again. As a long-time do-it-yourselfer, I know the pleasure of having the right tool for the job. And as you get better at using these particular tools, you will watch your relationship truly thrive.

THE POSSIBILITY:
REAL SELF,
TRUE CONNECTION

part one

The mind does not wish the best for you.
It is listening to the heart that will
lead you to happiness.

GAIL KALI

Would You Rather Be Right or Be Happy?

chapter 1

A couple airs their frustrations:

> "She just doesn't hear me. I try talk to her,
> and she doesn't listen."

> "I try to listen, but all I hear is how bad I am.
> It's better if I just stay away."

> "What happened to how things used to be?"

When we first get involved with someone, we generally experience some of the best feelings available to our human bodies and psyches. When we're in love, we have access to ecstasy. We are being seen for our best selves, and we're seeing our lover at his or her most wondrous. Both of us are enjoying the deep emotional and physical intimacy of sexuality that can be a mystical experience, bringing us to the heady aliveness of being completely in the moment as we touch into each other's divinity. All too often, however, this initial experience passes away (sometimes rather quickly) and is replaced by power struggle, conflict, and strife. The choice then seems to be to get used to life without ecstasy or to search it out elsewhere.

It is my belief and my experience that the passion, connection, and aliveness that are the hallmarks of new relationships are available no matter how long two people have been involved. In fact, I now expect to feel these things with my partner all the time, so that if we're not, it's a sign that action needs to be taken. In other words, if we're not feeling ease, flow, and aliveness (that is, *happy*) in our relationship, our internal alarms go off, and we take the actions to move back to that state.

Try out the idea that your natural state, your true essential self, is relaxed, open, curious, tuned in, and in harmonious flow with the universe. You're a river, just happily rolling along. Then, as occurs in life, *something happens.*[2] Someone cuts you off in traffic; you get an overdue notice; your dog gets sick; your partner says she's bored in the relationship. Suddenly the ease becomes constriction, your view of life narrows, and you have the sensation of life falling in on you. It seems like someone else's fault. You feel dammed up and begin to swirl in an eddy of confusion and stuckness.

Moving from ease to constriction is what happens when our brains get triggered. Relationship offers the precious gift of illuminating the triggers that we'd assumed were just part of us, so we can move through them and back into the ecstatic energy that life offers. This workbook is basically about how to notice the triggers, move through them, and come back into ease and aliveness. I believe it is possible to become conscious of triggers, to nonjudgmentally acknowledge them, then to choose a new path back to an open heart. I believe conscious relationship allows us all to choose love.

Most people want passionate, connected relationships where they can show up and be seen, known, and loved for who they really are. Is that true for you? It may come as a surprise to find out that closeness, connection, passion, and authenticity require you to be connected to your *body.* It sure was a shock to me. I was so used to relying on my mind, I had no idea why I didn't feel connected to my partner. It might sound a little strange, in this culture that emphasizes mind over matter, but what I've found is that my mind tends to be very unhelpful when it comes to moving through conflict. Following the wisdom of my body, though, allows me to get to the real issue quickly, and back to heartfelt connection.

Deep intimacy requires curiosity, wonder, and the ability to find the truth of one's experience deep in one's body. That might sound like a tall order, for those of us who were raised with the importance of being "reasonable" or who, perhaps, have honed our debate capabilities. Unfortunately, being great at arguing the fine points or keeping our feelings to ourselves takes us in absolutely the wrong direction. Scoring points, even winning the argument, might provide a momentary sense of satisfaction, but the thrill of competition sours in the wreckage of someone finally being declared the loser. (Once, while on a road trip, I argued with my partner through the entire state of Nebraska. While making the trip seem faster, it did nothing to resolve the issue or create intimacy.)

The hard habit to break is that of *arguing.* Arguing is a sign that we're in our heads, out of our bodies. Arguing is about beliefs, ideas, thoughts, and stories. It disconnects people. It's the opposite of being intimate.

So, get ready for a whole new way of being. Here is how it works. Keep breathing—it's a big step.

Anytime we make a statement that is arguable, that is, a statement that is about right or wrong, or good or bad, we have moved out of connection with our deepest, most essential selves. We argue over beliefs, and beliefs come from our conditioning, from what we've been taught by other people about how to live. Our true selves exist beyond what we've been taught to believe. Our essential nature is inborn. Intimacy happens when we're able to connect from one true self to another.

Here's the moment for a crucial choice. It comes down to this:

Would you rather be right or be happy?

Consider some examples of choosing to be *right:*

"I can't ever get a word in edgeways with you."

"You are such a slob."

"I am such a jerk."

"This will never get better."

"People are so thoughtless."

"Why are you always late?
 You're so inconsiderate and disrespectful."

"You never really cared about me."

Each of these statements invites agreement or disagreement. They are proclamations that pull for debate, where evidence must be produced to reach a verdict: Who is really right? And, more importantly, who is wrong? It is the mind at work, analyzing, judging, and compiling data.

Intimate connection never happens at the level of mind.

Perhaps a moment of bonding occurs if we agree with each other, but that isn't true intimacy, it's the knitting together of allies against a common enemy: Yes, we understand each other; we understand how the world works. What a relief! Of course, if there is disagreement, there is no possibility for even that brief moment of relief. Ongoing power struggles and stuckness in relationship are generally the outcome of two people trying to work out issues through the right-wrong strategy. This strategy actually can become toxic over time, as these debates have a way of escalating into character attack and counterattack. The conflict can easily slide from whose action or belief is right or wrong, to whose *self* is right or wrong:

"You're supposed to turn here."

"No, it's up ahead."

"Why don't you ever listen to me?"

"I would, if you were ever right."

"I was right last week when I got us to the concert."

"Oh, sure, that we had to race to because you were late again."

"I wouldn't have been late if I hadn't had to finish the bills that you said you were going to do. You never do what you say you're going to do."

"Who could follow through on anything with someone nagging at them all the time!"

"Oh, so now I'm a nag."

One reason that the beginning of a relationship feels so wonderful is that each person is seen for the very best of who she or he is. We feel we are with, or we are, the most beautiful, smartest, most considerate person alive. It's what being in love is all about. As differences inevitably occur, however, and we try to debate our way out of them using logic and trying to win the fight, the gloss begins to wear off. Escalating arguments lead to the use of blaming labels. The other is now too thoughtless, needy, lazy, cold, slow, fast, obsessive, irresponsible. Too emotional, too rational. Too something. Our initial experience of ourselves and our loved one as truly amazing beings begins to shift to what is wrong. "You're so caring!" becomes "People take advantage of you." "You are brilliantly creative" turns into "I can't believe how much you sit around staring at the wall." "I love how physically affectionate you are!" degrades into "You only want sex. Why are you so demanding?"

While we might initially respond to this new negative view of ourselves by trying to behave better, it takes effort. We get tired. The new relationship just doesn't feel as good, as we no longer feel cherished for who we are. We start to defend ourselves, which can turn into escalation and counterattack. Frustrated by our inability to find the wonderful feelings we used to have, we might try harder to use the main tool we have—debate—which takes us to the same dead ends. Ultimately, we may simply try to avoid the conflict altogether, choosing to shut down. And we wonder: whatever happened to feeling in love?

So, what is the alternative? How in the world do we create something different? What can take us out of the downward spin into negativity to resolution of the issue and deeper connection?

Here is a passageway to a whole new way of relating:

Speak from your heart, from your deepest self, from the only *unarguable* truth there really is: *what is going on inside your body.*

Your Commitments

We'll work more with the skill of shifting to unarguable statements in a bit. But first, as the Hendricks say, any change requires commitment.[3]

Did anybody feel scared about the *c word?* You might want to take a breath. What I mean by commitment here is to get clear about how you are organizing your energy. Because how

TOOL TRY IT OUT

Get out your journal. Take a breath and notice your inner world. What statements can you make that are based on what is going on inside your body and completely unarguable? Now, can you make any statements about the exterior world and what is going on outside of you that someone couldn't argue with?

Here are some examples of arguable statements, and how to shift them into being unarguable:

Arguable	Unarguable
It's cold in here.	I feel cold.
You're a slob.	I don't like clothes on the floor.
The world is a mess.	I feel scared about what is happening in the world, and I don't know what action to take.
You don't understand me.	I'm afraid that I'm not making myself clear.

you organize your energy will determine the results you get. As I use the word *commitment* through this book, I'm really wanting you to become conscious of how you're currently organizing your energy and then what you might want to do differently.

So before we really go into some transformational tools, I'd like you to try out some commitments. Speak them out loud and see what they feel like in your body. Proclaim them to the world—or at least, to your partner. Though truly, the commitments you make are between you and you (or, if you like, between you and the universe).

Here's a hint for being able to tell if you're on the right track with your commitments: your body will feel more open, alive, and expanded, versus more shutdown, closed, and contracted.

OK, here's the old commitment for many of us:

> "I commit to being right at all costs, and to winning instead of losing—whatever it takes."

What does that feel like? Does your body feel open, expanded, good, or more contracted and closed?

Now, try these out:

> "I commit to being open to learning from every relationship interaction. I commit to knowing my deepest, most authentic self and to communicating who I am impeccably to others."

If you actually prefer the commitment to being right, I recommend you close this book now (though if you find a way to happiness through that avenue, I'd certainly like to hear about it). If the commitment to your authenticity gives you a sense of juiciness and possibility, you are on the road that I've found to be endlessly engaging, challenging, and rewarding.

Your commitments propel you forward to a whole new set of possibilities. Making the commitment directs you to the *what;* now we'll start working on the *how.*

TOOL   COMMITTING TO HAPPINESS

Now it's your turn. What commitments would you like to make to support yourself on a new path? Write these down in your journal and refer back to them whenever you lose connection to your commitments.

I commit to

And

Speaking the Unarguable Truth

chapter 2

If someone is arguing with you,
you are saying something arguable.

Speaking the unarguable truth is the most powerful of any of the skills I have to teach you and, from my own experience, the most challenging. It is a simple concept, yet is foreign enough to most of us to be anything but easy. We've been raised to think critically, to debate concepts, beliefs, and ideas. Then we get into relationships, where these skills take us straight into escalation and disconnection. Shifting into speaking unarguably can feel like trying to grow a new limb. But it will allow you to walk through life in true partnership and intimacy.

Many of us have some notion that we should bring feelings into our conversations and that other people don't get to tell us how to feel. However, this basic idea tends to run us aground, sounding something like this:

"I feel like you are attacking me."

"I feel that this is going nowhere."

If someone is arguing with you, you are saying something arguable.

"I am sad and hurt that you just don't consider me."

Can you argue with these statements? Remember, if you can, they're arguable. That's all it takes (and I can for sure argue with each of these sentences). So let's take this idea of unarguability further.

The goal of moving from arguable to unarguable statements is to get away from blaming and to shift into fully owning, and actually having, one's experience. When we say arguable things, we are projecting our past experiences onto the other person. Occasionally we're accurate, but for the most part, our projections are wildly off the mark and apt to just pull the other person into whatever old issue we haven't worked out yet. When we can actually observe these projections for what they are, we have a ticket into healing old wounds: as we watch ourselves get triggered into acting out the old scenarios from our childhood with our partners, it actually becomes possible to move them out of our bodies. Unfortunately, we generally believe our own projections, and then get our partners to be our co-stars in our old unconscious dramas.

Speaking the unarguable truth takes us beyond our projections to the only provable truth there is: our own experience. While we can never be completely sure of what's going on outside of our bodies (Is that person really mad at us? Is the economy good or bad? Is that tone rude or too loud or too sharp?), we *know* that our stomach feels tight or that our jaw is clenched. The skill here is to *only speak what we truly know.*

So, what is unarguable? Truly, the only thing that someone else can't argue about is what we are sensing in our bodies, that is, whether we have butterflies in our chest or a headache or a dry mouth. I'm going to take it a step further and add that no one gets to argue with *what we are feeling* or with *what we want.* So that's the list of what is unarguable: sensations, emotions, and what we want.

Sensations

What is a sensation you're having right now? Is your throat dry, your chest open, your jaw clenched? (And did you ever think anyone would even think that's something important to ask about?)

Sensations are our body's way of getting our attention. They provide the first line of communication between our body and our mind, as our body zings a contraction here; a bubbling there; a pain, an openness, a warmth, or a tightness to try to communicate with us. In fact, sensations are the bridge between our essential self and our awareness. They are the main detour around what we're taught to believe and back to who we really are.

With our culture's emphasis on being rational, it might seem odd to start to listen to these cues that our body is sending out. However, being able to discern and then communicate what sensations you are having from moment to moment will help you, and those around you, know what is truly going on for you.

TOOL   DESCRIBE YOUR SENSATIONS

Close your eyes and breathe in. Take an inventory of your body sensations from head to toe. What do you notice? Look for sensations such as contraction, openness, relaxation, tightness, clenching, buzzing, aching, warmth, expansion, frozenness, fast/slow/deep/shallow breathing, dizziness, heaviness, lightness, calm. List what you notice in your journal.

Emotions

How do you imagine that a body tells us what it is feeling? Indeed, by what sensations it is having. So emotions are next on the list of what is unarguable.

It can be challenging to translate sensations into the actual emotions being generated, but as you get to know your body, it will get easier and easier to know what it is trying to tell you. I find it helpful to keep this very simple and to focus on using just the primary emotions. Psychologists and anthropologists argue about which are truly the most primary, universal emotions. I suggest these:

mad,   sad,   scared,   glad,   sexual.

Notice what is not on the list: slightly perplexed, annoyed, hopeless, confused, fine, depressed, anxious, or shut down. All of those states are actually a primary emotion plus a whole lot of thoughts added into it. I want you to be able to tune into the most basic of your emotions without distancing from them by interpreting them through your mind (as this is where projection begins).

OK, so now we're on an unarguable roll. We start with:

"I notice (a body sensation)."

Then we add the emotion:

"I feel (mad/sad/scared/glad/sexual)."

Try it out. Look at your list of sensations you came up with a few minutes ago, and see if you can link each sensation to an emotion. This could sound like: "I notice that my stomach feels clenched up. I feel scared." Or "I notice my body is relaxed and buzzy. I feel open, expanded—glad."

mad
sad
scared
glad
sexual

So far, so good. But what if we want to add a description to this, a "because . . . "?

Notice that the further we get from the actual sensation, the more iffy our whole statement becomes. We might be accurate in describing our own experience; we might not. But if we choose to go there, the same rule applies: *the whole statement needs to be unarguable.* It's helpful to distinguish between how I feel (unarguable) and what my thoughts, images, beliefs or judgments are.

Try these ideas out with the following statement:

> "I notice tightness in my solar plexus. I feel scared
>   and mad because you're driving too fast."

That was a good start but shifted to a crashing finish (hopefully not), becoming arguable. (Do you hear the blame in it? That's the main sign of getting off track.)

Here's an unarguable version:

> "I feel tight all over and sick to my stomach.
>   I'm clutching the seat. I have images of having a big
>   accident. I feel really scared."

Do you see how the blame drops away? If there's no attack, there's no need to defend, enabling connection, understanding, and mutual support. And we get to really be seen for the actual experience we're having. Right in the moment. Our vulnerability becomes our strength, as the other can see us and hear us. And maybe we'll even get what we want.

Let's practice the first two steps of speaking the unarguable truth, sensations and emotions. Then we'll add the icing on the cake: what we want or don't want.

TOOL   MOVING FROM THE ARGUABLE TO THE UNARGUABLE (SENSATIONS AND EMOTIONS)

Convert the following into unarguable, nonblaming statements, focusing on the sensations and emotions that go with these statements. (You can find some possible answers to these statements in appendix 2.)

Arguable: You are always late.

Unarguable:

Arguable: They are really ignorant.

Unarguable:

Arguable: My life sucks.

Unarguable:

Arguable: I'm bad.

Unarguable:

Arguable: Your friends don't like me.

Unarguable:

Arguable: My boss is always criticizing me. He doesn't appreciate me.

Unarguable:

Arguable: You don't love me.

Unarguable:

Arguable: This will never work.

Unarguable:

What You Want

The final part of making an effective unarguable statement is to add *what you want.*

When we're really tuned into our bodies, they will tell us pretty unequivocally what they want. Our minds are much less trustworthy in this area, as they often confuse what they want with what they *should* want, or with what others tell them to want. This can lead to trying to justify what we want with a bunch of data or support from others, or having to debate over whose wants are more legitimate. There's that pesky mind again, hoping to be right and creating disconnection in its wake.

I like the idea that people get to want what they want, just because they want it. Try that out: you get to want what you want for no other reason than you want it. (This was a revolutionary idea for me and one that has cleared away much of my depression. Between the "shoulds" I was living from and my unwillingness to be clear about what I wanted, my life didn't reflect much of me.) And you get to not want it because you don't want it. Does this mean you always get your way? Maybe, once you get really good at making agreements (see chapter 14). But even if you don't, you do have the space to speak what you want or don't want and know those things are valid.

Notice that this approach drops away any need for justifying what you want or don't want. You don't have to prove why you're right to want to leave this boring party or not go to the difficult in-laws for the holidays. Saying "because I want to (or don't want to)" is a good enough reason. Suddenly, much of the material for conflict just falls away.

You also may find that when you give yourself full permission to have what you want or not have what you don't want, there is space for the deeper, more relevant issues to surface. What you initially think you want (e.g., to pay the bills on time, to not be late) may give way to the underlying wants that you weren't even aware of (e.g., be on the same team, live from flow, feel loved).

Many people have unlearned their natural ability to know what they want. Past disappointments may have taught them that it's better to not want anything. Or they grew up in families that helped them disconnect their inner wants from outer circumstances: "You shouldn't be hungry. We just ate dinner," or (my experience) "Girls don't play the trumpet. Pick another instrument." So letting yourself know what you want could be a whole new exploration. Here are some tips for unearthing what you really want:

> » Often we know what we *don't want* first. That's a fine place to begin.
> » Wanting happens *in your body*. It's one of the ways your body is reliable. Take some breaths, walk around, and see if ideas about what you really want pop up from somewhere besides your mind.
> » Practice what *yes* and *no* feel like in your body. For many folks, *yes* is an open, energized sensation, especially in their chest and solar plexus. *No* might feel more closed and shutdown, a flat feeling.

TOOL   CALIBRATING YOUR YES AND YOUR NO

Get out your journal, as you'll want access to this valuable tool later.

Imagine your very favorite food, music, or activity. What sensations do you notice in your body?

My Yes Signals:

Now imagine the most ghastly food, music, or activity you can think of.
What sensations do you notice in your body?

My No Signals:

TOOL   UNEARTHING WHAT YOU REALLY WANT AND DON'T WANT

Over the next few days, practice figuring out what you really want. Slow down and be sure you're giving yourself time to decide things such as
> what you want to eat,
> what you want to do with your free time (from moments to hours),
> what music you want to listen to, and
> who you want to spend your time with.

Journal about what you've learned. Are you able to discern what you want and what you don't want? What do you notice has helped you to do that?

S.E.W.

Now you have all of the ingredients to speak an unarguable truth: sensations, emotions, and what you want. So let's go back to the example we were working on before, about driving in the car. (I've had the fantasy of doing a research project on the freeway, randomly pulling cars over to find out which couples are arguing. There's something about driving together that can really get a conflict going.)

Here's the full, unarguable statement:

> "I feel tight all over and sick to my stomach. I'm clutching the seat. I'm having images of being in a big accident. I feel really scared. I want to feel safe. My request is that you slow down."

What do you think? Can you imagine talking this way? I do—and I sure do enjoy driving with my partner now.

An acronym that might help you remember how to speak in an unarguable way is S.E.W.

Sensations, Emotions, Want

Let's use S.E.W. to try to work our way through a different, common conflict couples have: who does the housework. Notice how using S.E.W. will take us completely away from a blaming statement and back into connection and flow through the unarguable truth.

> *Blaming:* "I hate it when my partner never helps with the housework. He's so inconsiderate and doesn't help around the house. I swear he never had to grow up. He always had someone to wait on him, and I'm not about to do that."

How does your body feel, just reading that? As I wrote that I felt pretty tensed up. So let's all feel better and ask the speaker to speak using S.E.W.

> *Sensations:* "I feel tightness in my chest, and my throat feels closed up. There's shooting pain in my temples."

> *Emotions:* "I feel fear in my chest, sadness in my throat, and anger in my temples. I feel afraid. I feel sad. I feel angry."

> *Want:* "What I really want is a clean house. Actually, now that I sit with all of this, what I really want is a sense of control. Hmmm, there's more below that. I want to feel more flow with my partner and more ease about our agreements."

Thoughts anchor. Feelings flow!

Are you starting to see how this works?

As I mentioned earlier, of any of the skills I have to teach you, I view speaking the unarguable truth as the most powerful. It has changed my life and literally all of my relationships to be able to get down to what is really going on for me. And since I've practiced this quite a lot over time, I find that now I can get to the unarguable truth in just a few moments.

In any situation of conflict, shifting to the bottom-line, most internal truth moves what was stuck (thoughts, beliefs, ideas) into the arena of what can move, that is, emotions. While thoughts anchor an experience, feelings flow (which is how "e-motions" are supposed to work—energy in motion).

Thoughts anchor. Feelings flow!

People are often surprised, once they've really listened to themselves, about what truths surface. And once they know their own truth, they can find connection with themselves, create connection with the other, and ultimately take actions to shift the issue. Meanwhile, speaking the unarguable truth allows for the other to actually listen without having to defend him- or herself. The blame drops out, leaving the heart of the speaker's experience to be fully heard. Suddenly it is possible to be allies—two people who have communicated clearly, who now can work together as a team to find solutions to the issue.

Though speaking the unarguable truth is simple and basic, I don't want to mislead you; I have not found it to be easy. Speaking in an unarguable way means giving up blame, and blaming can be a hard habit to break. It is so clear to us that we were feeling fine a moment ago, and then they said that mean thing or came home late or forgot our birthday, and now we're upset. The logic seems inescapable: they did this to us.

What may not make so much sense to us is how we're actually the source of whatever we're experiencing. In fact, you could say we're all walking around as triggers waiting to happen. Past traumas and old hurts come to the surface when we feel threatened and when that unexpected something happens. When we choose to notice our sensations and emotions, and then take the risk to say what we really want, we quickly can get to the heart of what our bodies are trying most to tell us and move the old, accumulated energies through. Speaking what is happening for us in an unarguable way allows those around us to stay openhearted, compassionate, and calm while they ride through our upset with us.

I used to be a master at the arguable. Blaming seemed like the only smart way to be (sort of like the best defense is a good offense). But I found that the moment of being right was not at all worth what followed: suffering, unhappiness, discord. Now I know what a revolutionary act it is to have a relationship that is free of blame. Knowing that we are the source of our experience marks a significant shift in consciousness, as we discover what our essential selves are trying to communicate and let those around us see who we really are.

TOOL   TRACKING AND TRANSLATING THE ARGUABLE

Take a day to listen for the arguable statements you speak, hear, think, and read around you. Write some of these down in your journal and translate them into unarguable statements.

Arguable:

Unarguable:

Arguable:

Unarguable:

Arguable:

Unarguable:

Arguable:

Unarguable:

TOOL   SHIFTING A CONFLICT

Remember a conflict that you had recently (or better yet, one that you're in the middle of).
Start with all the blaming, judgmental statements you have in your mind. Write them in your journal.

Now, look carefully at how each statement is arguable.

Next, take a few good, deep breaths, and get ready to shift these into *unarguable* statements.

Read the first statement and answer the following questions:

1. What sort of sensations do you notice in your body?

2. What emotions (mad, sad, scared, glad, sexual) are associated with these sensations?

3. List some of the thoughts or images that come up for you. Do these remind you of anything?

4. Finally, what is it that you *really* want?

(It is possible that you'll need to go through questions 1–4 with all of your statements, but it is likely they all point to the same bottom line.)

LISTENING TO YOUR BODY

part two

Anyone gets to feel anything,
anytime, for any reason.

Understanding the Five Basic Emotions

Did anyone ever sit down and tell you how emotions work? We learn about math and social studies in school, but how many of us had any education at all in the mysterious world of feelings? (Even though I went through five years of graduate school in psychology, we spent not one minute discussing how emotions work.)

Even if you believe you are quite competent in this area, there may indeed be some surprises for you in this chapter. And for those of you who go blank when your intimate partner says, "tell me how you *feel* about this," emotions are actually quite logical, if you understand how they function.

For most of us, there is a constant dance between the mind and the body. Much of what we say that we *feel* is really what we *think*. "I feel you are being unfair." "I feel scared that you just don't get it." "I feel stupid." It's a habit. Many of the words that sound like emotions have thoughts mixed in. Disappointment tends to be anger plus fear plus a thought, for example, "I'll never get what I want." Other words we use—such as confused, perplexed, and misunderstood—are actually mostly thoughts, like "I don't get it," or "you're not making sense," or "why aren't you *listening to me!*" (And notice how the thoughts tend to be blaming judgments.) "I feel hurt" really means, "I think it's your fault that interaction went badly." And a favorite for many of us, "I feel bad," is really mind-code for something like "I think I'm unacceptable to you," or "I have no idea what I'm feeling."

The trick is to come down into the body and out of the mind, over and over and over. The truth is in the body. The way to recognize it is its unarguability and how it resonates deep within: *Yes! That's true!*

Emotions have information; when we pay attention to them, they give us useable data (which could be a comfort for those of you who might believe that the whole "feeling thing" is too airy-fairy).

I want to take a moment to highlight a very confusing aspect of having an emotion. We are typically backward about figuring out what is its source. When an emotion happens, our first response is usually to look for who or what outside of us caused it. Maybe we were feeling good until the guy cut us off in traffic, so we blame the guy for being an inconsiderate #$%&*. Or we were having a quiet time until our spouse came home and started telling us about her lousy day at work, resulting in our feeling fear and anger. Or we're walking along and see someone that we judge to be gorgeous, and we suddenly have sexual feelings.

In each of these situations, it might appear that the other person is the source of emotion. However,

We are the source of what we are feeling.

we are the source of what we are feeling.

Yep, always. It's our body that's lighting up, clenching, racing, freezing, exploding. We're the source of the emotional experience, not the other person. As logical as it seems ("I didn't feel this until you did that"), it throws us way off track when we see others as the reason we're feeling what we're feeling. Once we know our emotions are all about us—they actually have little or nothing to do with the other—we can intervene where it makes the most sense. With our own bodies.

Do you see what a time-saver this is? That means instead of having to control the entire world—or maybe just your partner—so you don't have to feel something you don't want to feel, you just have to focus on you. Like the person who decided to just put on shoes instead of having to cover the world in leather, you bring your power back when you know that you are the source of your emotions.

Before we jump into the world of emotion, there is an important idea I'd like you to stop and breathe into.

Anyone gets to feel anything, anytime, for any reason.

Anything. Anytime. For *any* reason. (This will help immensely down the road. Trust me.)

OK, so are you ready to learn more about what emotions are trying to tell you? I'll walk you through each of the five primary emotions and give you the key information you need to fully understand and interpret the main points of your inner world.

There are hundreds of words in the dictionary for emotions. I find it to be very helpful to stay with the five basic emotions of mad, sad, scared, glad, and sexual while getting to know this work (though, truly, I pretty much stick to these five myself). Each of these is a pure, physiological reaction that all mammals have. Compare this to other words people use to describe their emotions, like *disappointed, hurt,* or *anxious.* Once you veer away from the primary emotions, you are likely to start bringing thought—and arguability—into the conversation. Like the big crayons that are the primary colors, noticing these primary emotions will take you right into your body to the real issue that is trying to get your attention. And remember, finding the real issue means finding the real, essential you.

Anyone gets to feel anything, anytime, for any reason.

Mad

Anger tries to get our attention through sensations that mostly show up as tightness or contraction in our neck, jaw, shoulders, and lower back. Clenched fists and headaches are also anger signals. Anger energy wants to move out of the body. Growling, pushing against, twisting something, and stomping our feet can satisfy this need for expression.

From a physiological perspective, anger occurs for two reasons: when we're stopping an *intrusion* and when we are trying to get through an *obstacle*. It is an instant uprising of energy to push through what was stopping us (Omph!) or to stop what is coming through (No!). In other words,

> pure, nonblaming anger is a signal that we are getting what we don't want (experiencing an intrusion) or not getting what we want (experiencing an obstacle).

Notice that experiencing an intrusion or an obstacle actually has nothing to do with anyone else; it's yours alone. Yes, this is the part where "you are the source." Because if you can really take that idea in, you'll make a key move to taking your power back. When you're mad, it's because you're mad! It's your experience of the intrusion or obstacle. This is your boundary, your self, your being. Not someone else's. You get to have a boundary or say you want something just because that's part of how you know you're you.

In other words, just because you're angry doesn't mean you get to blame someone else. But you do get to feel it.

I wish it were more socially acceptable for adults to have tantrums. That would be a much clearer expression of "I'm not getting what I want" or "I'm getting what I don't want." (Can you imagine how much this would clarify road rage? "I wanted to go first! I didn't want *you* to go first! Wah!")

The activation that comes from trying to move through the obstacle or to stop the intrusion can feel really big. And the heat of

Pure, nonblaming anger is a signal that we are getting what we don't want (experiencing an intrusion) or not getting what we want (experiencing an obstacle).

anger seems to be looking for a target, that is, something or someone to blame. As a result there are endless examples of anger being used destructively, through criticism and verbal or physical attack. Having experienced this destructiveness, many people decide to simply turn off the energy, and not let themselves be angry. The consequence to this off-switch is that they find they can't feel any of the big energies, like passion or sexuality or life-force. Using anger well, that is, using it as *power* instead of as destructiveness, can require lots of practice to reach mastery of this intense energy.

Blaming anger is attack. Blameless anger is sheer power, a lightning bolt of energy that we can use productively. Speaking one's anger without blame can be the most challenging of the unarguable truth statements:

"I feel angry because you're late." The arguability of this can be found in the underlying blaming of this statement.

"I feel angry because I didn't get to eat dinner when I was planning to." Now we're coming back to actual power, the power that comes from clarity. And notice how this will direct this person to the next step, the *W* of the S.E.W.? *"So what I want is to eat when I'm hungry. I'm not going to wait for you."*

Want to try it again with intrusion, the part of anger about getting what we don't want? Here's a typical arguable, blaming, attacking statement: *"I'm over it! You're never satisfied!"* How about this: *"I feel angry that you always want sex!"* Not much better, is it? Then we have: *"I notice my jaw is clenched. I feel angry. I don't want to have sex."* Pretty clear, isn't it?

Here's one last comment about anger before we move on: anger can be a sign of not making clear agreements, that is, not making sure we get what we want. If we have made unclear agreements (or never made any agreements at all), there will often be a percolating sense of anger under the surface, as things feel energetically out of whack to us. As with all the emotions, tuning in to the information that the anger is trying to deliver, for example, that new agreements need to be made, will allow the anger to finish its job of communicating to you, and move on through.

Sad

Sadness can often be spotted as heaviness in the chest, tightness in the throat, and tearing in the eyes. It is a pure physiological signal that we have *lost* something or someone that we felt attached to.

Sadness is a signal that we are experiencing loss.

Sadness is a signal that we are experiencing loss.

In other words, sad feelings occur across a spectrum, from the everyday losses of breaking a treasured object or not being invited to a party, to the profound losses of a job or relationship, or the death of a loved one. Allowing the experience of sadness to well up and move through is really about taking the time to honor the importance of what was lost and to say our goodbyes. Allowing full expression, from slow tear leakage to all-out sobbing, supports the clearing out of sadness.

Sadness is an emotion that seems to particularly frighten people, with the idea that "if I let myself cry, I may never stop." Tuning into current sadness can connect us with any past losses that we never let ourselves fully experience, until we may feel as though we're drowning in a bottomless pool of grief. Allowing yourself full expression of your sadness for as long as it takes can be a huge gift to yourself. You'll find that you will, indeed, find solid ground again, and with it new confidence in your ability to surf huge emotional waves.

Scared

Low-grade fear might appear as butterflies in the solar plexus or stomach; as it increases, the whole body is affected, as it goes into the fight-flight-freeze response. Agitation, muscle tension, increased pulse and blood pressure, and shallow breathing are all signals of fear that has generalized to the whole body. Effective expression of fear can include shaking and quaking, running (literally letting yourself run away from what is scaring you), and letting yourself notice how frightened your body actually is.

We feel fear when there is a perceived *threat* to our physical or emotional well-being.

Fear is a signal that we are perceiving a threat.

Fear as a physiological response gets us to pay close attention to our surroundings and prepare for an action, stay and fight, or turn around and flee. If the threat becomes too overwhelming, we are likely to go into a freeze or faint response, where we feel paralyzed and unable to act at all.

Animals in the wild are better off fleeing than fighting, as fighting places them at risk for injury or death.[4]

Glad

The emotion of glad feels expanded, warm, flowing, and connected. Glad feelings can happen anywhere in the body, though they generally begin in the chest and heart area.

Glad is a signal that we're experiencing well-being, safety, and connection.

There are two types of glad: glad that is peaceful, and glad that is excited. With peaceful glad, our muscles relax, our breathing slows, our vision expands, and we're able to access new, creative possibilities in our thinking. We often feel loving and deeply connected with ourselves, with others, and even with the universe. Peaceful glad might not even want expression; when it does the expression might be physical contact, or it might be some sort of expression that goes beyond language. Peaceful glad inspires art that connects us to what is most awesome about our world.

Fear is a signal that we are perceiving a threat.

Animals in the wild are better off fleeing than fighting, as fighting places them at risk for injury or death.

Excited glad tends to have more energy. It can feel buzzy and exhilarating throughout the body. Our pulse rises, our cheeks flush, and our muscles activate. Expression of excited glad is all about joyful and spontaneous movement, allowing our bodies to express what can truly be one of the best experiences we have of being human.

Sexual

Sexual feels like expanding heat. It generally begins in the genital area; it can stay localized there, or spread throughout the body.

> Sexual is a signal that we're experiencing
> arousal in our erogenous zones.

Expression of sexual feelings can be about stimulation and orgasm. However, sexual feelings are not just about wanting to have sex. That is far too limiting a definition. Instead, sexual energy is your creativity, your lust for life, your willingness to tune into all of your cells and notice whether they're numbed out or on fire or exhausted or recharged or in flow.

The huge flow of energy that is your aliveness can be *on* (with your attention, breath, movement, and willingness to speak what is unarguably true for you) or it can be *off* (as you distract yourself, stop moving and breathing deeply, and drift into arguability). If you've turned your energy off, you might be jarred into awareness by someone you can really talk to or someone with whom you can laugh or create. *But that other person is not the source of what you are feeling.* You are.

And, remember that part about "you are the source"? This idea is extremely important right here. Just as you are the source of feeling glad, feeling sexual feelings is all about you. As Gay Hendricks once said, "Under the right circumstances, we can all feel attracted to a rhododendron."[5]

Glad is a signal that we're experiencing well-being, safety, and connection.

Sexual is a signal that we're experiencing arousal in our erogenous zones.

People get confused about their sexual feelings, as it seems so clear that we feel sexual because of another person. It's completely logical, right? We look at someone, or touch, hug, kiss them, and feel sexual feelings, so they must be the reason our body is feeling aroused. Logical, but wrong.

The sensations are happening in our body. We weren't feeling them, and then we were. In other words, the sensations arise from us. We are the source.

This is a good time to take a breath and move around. This idea is completely different from the cultural message that we just have to find the right person to feel happy and to be sexually fulfilled. Many a relationship ends over this concept, so I want to be sure you understand what I mean. It's not about the pin-up girl or the gorgeous guy or the hot colleague at the office.

Your sexual feelings are all about you.

Note this about sexual: Remember how "anyone gets to feel anything, anytime, for any reason"? That includes all feelings, including sexual. In other words, you get to feel sexual (and mad, sad, scared, and glad) any time. With anybody. Because you do. *Acting on those feelings is a whole other story.* Just like you can feel angry without killing someone, you can feel sexual without having sex. Letting yourself fully experience every single emotion fully is truly letting yourself experience what your body is built for: your full aliveness.

This can be a pretty radical shift of perspective for folks. What if you could walk around feeling full flow, noticing your sexual feelings and sensations here, and your anger there. Maybe you're talking to one person and noticing how your body shifts through the kaleidoscope of fear and sadness and gladness and sexuality, or another where you mostly notice the irritability of anger. And you breathe through it all, without deciding something like, "Wow, I don't feel this when I'm around my partner, so that means I should be with this person instead." Or "I have to make sure I'm never around that person ever again." What if you fully embraced that your body is a river of emotion that constantly moves through you, without it actually meaning much of anything at all?

Moving into the expanded states of glad and sexual often becomes more possible once the denser energies of mad, sad, and scared have moved through. People in relationships often wonder why they no longer feel "in love" or attracted to their partners. If they are unwilling to feel more difficult feelings, these more positive energies become unavailable as well. The body doesn't operate with different switches that can be turned off and on according to which emotions are acceptable to us. Instead, we only have one big switch that turns off everything—or turns everything back on. That means to find these big and wonderful feelings of sexuality and gladness, we must be willing to experience and move the more difficult ones.

TOOL   FROM SENSATIONS TO EMOTIONS

Carry your journal around with you for a day. Set an alarm to go off once an hour. Jot down your sensations and see if you can translate them into which of the five emotions you are feeling.

Sensations   **Emotion**

TOOL TRANSLATING YOUR EMOTIONS

This exercise will give you a big payoff in your ability to track your emotions and what they are trying to tell you. The more you practice, the better you'll be able to translate your emotions' messages. Carry your journal around for several days for this exercise; you may be surprised at what your body is trying to tell you.

Translation Key
- » Anger: Intrusion/Obstacle
- » Sadness: Loss
- » Fear: Threat
- » Glad: Well-Being
- » Sexual: Arousal/Creativity

Sensations	Emotion	Message

Feeling Too Good

chapter 4

Something to watch for in experiencing the more expanded states of glad and sexual is how most of us have trouble feeling very good for very long. Gay and Kathlyn Hendricks label this the "upper limits problem,"[6] believing this to be the only *real* problem that there is in relationship (as everything else can be moved through quickly and easily by speaking the truth and taking responsibility for one's experience).

Because we human beings aren't that practiced at feeling really good (versus those states we've truly mastered: mad, sad, and scared), we tend to interrupt our sensations of expansion and feeling wonderful by getting sick or injured, starting an argument, or getting cranky. We're like balloons that inflate to our limit of previous experience and then need to learn how to tolerate that level of expansion by resting before we can get even bigger.

According to Katie Hendricks, most of us can stand feeling good for about four seconds.[7]

According to Katie Hendricks, most of us can stand feeling good for about four seconds.

Contrast this pattern:

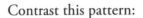

with what we typically seem to expect in life and relationships:

The key to shifting to the top pattern is knowing when we need to take time to rest and regroup—and actually taking it.

There is another consequence of feeling expanded and wonderful that I've noticed that I want to draw your attention to. When we feel the open and expanded energies of glad and sexual, the very energy of our spacious bodies seems to draw forth old, contracted energies of mad, sad, and scared that we haven't previously allowed ourselves to process. In other words, past experiences of emotions that were too big for you to feel way back when were stored away in your energy body. Feeling spacious and alive literally draws out those unprocessed emotions into the more expanded energy field of feeling really good. If you can really grasp this idea, you'll be much more able to ride whatever emotion comes up, no matter when you feel it. Having creative ways to handle the Upper Limits Problem is a gateway to a happier, more fulfilled, and easeful life. Giving your body lots of time and space to learn how to feel increasingly wonderful (and whatever else that brings with it) will allow you to experience a whole new aspect of life, one where flow, magic, and new possibilities reign.

TOOL   UPPER LIMITS AND REST

Use your journal to answer the following questions: What are your signals that you've reached your upper limit?

What do you do for rest and to replenish yourself? Are you giving yourself these things?

TOOL   UPPER LIMIT DETECTION

Get out your journal and consider the last time you had some relationship glitches and conflicts. As you muse about what happened, can you:

» Remember feeling really good, open, or expanded before the problem occurred?

» See old feelings or issues that arose from the problem that you haven't fully addressed?

» Notice that you needed rest?

Emotions: Energy in Motion

chapter 5

You just downloaded a whole bunch of information about emotions in the prior chapters. Do you see how truly logical they are? Emotions are such an exquisite communication system. We're going along in our lives, and something happens. Immediately our bodies signal us through particular sensations so we'll know if there's an intrusion, an obstacle, a loss, a threat, a reason to appreciate or celebrate, or an attraction. Actually listening to what your body is trying—sometimes desperately—to communicate with you can change your experience of your inner world from one of complicated mystery to one of clarity and understanding. You'll know yourself, and you'll be able to communicate who you really are to anyone, anytime. For any reason.

The work of conscious relationship relies on being able to tune into one's body and know what it is trying to communicate. That is, to get beyond what the mind thinks is correct (*I shouldn't be angry right now—there is nothing to really be angry about. So I guess I'm not.*) and discover the truth of what the body is really saying. Stuckness in relationship—that is, those times when all movement forward has ground to a halt, with both (or all) people completely embroiled in power struggle—happens because *emotions* are stuck. That might seem farfetched right now, as it certainly can appear that conflict happens over more concrete disagreements. But haven't you wondered how something as trivial as how the toilet paper hangs from the roller can turn into such a battle? Even the most important issues could probably be solved relatively easily if people didn't get emotionally triggered along the way.

Note about "Emotional People" Versus "Rational People"

We tend to divide people into those who are extra emotional and those who are more on the rational end of the spectrum. We even have ideas that one gender is able to feel or express more, while another just thinks their way through.

I don't buy it. Having worked with all combinations of genders in intimate relationships, I see how one person might hoist the flag of "I understand how emotions work and you don't" and the other might view him- or herself as reasonable and cool. However, what I notice is that very few folks know what is really going on under their own skin. As a species, we've just recently started to map out the emotional world and understand how to interface with it.

I also notice that "emotional people" tend to use the words *I feel* at the beginning of their sentences and get lost into the blame of arguability pretty fast. "I feel like you don't understand me—but it's my feeling, so you don't get to argue with me!" is a common drift out of emotions and into thoughts. (Pop quiz: Make that statement unarguable.)

Finally, I think under that rational, cool exterior is often a bubbling volcano of sensation. (One of the few gender differences that stands up to scrutiny is that men feel conflict more intensely than women.[8]) What I hear in sessions are statements like, "I don't know how I feel. But I do have stomach problems all the time."

My invitation is to let yourself be a beginner about the vast world of your emotional landscape, even if you think you're an expert. Let yourself start from the basics so you and your partner (or other buddy in this learning) can try out these ideas, and fail, and try again, maybe even laugh and encourage each other with love along the way.

Riding the Waves

Lack of mastery of internal states is behind so many of our personal difficulties. We might say we're "anxious" or "depressed." But we generally feel clueless as to how our anxiety relates to the agitation we're experiencing in our body, what started it, or how to manage it. Depression can result from our ongoing "depressing" of our feelings, generally because we don't know what else to do with them. Since early childhood, most of us have had many, many experiences of feeling emotionally overwhelmed. Without support about how to move these big feelings through our bodies, many of us are experts on how to automatically shut them down. Every time we manage this rather Herculean feat of turning off our sensations, we add another layer of stuck energy to our bodies. By adulthood, there can be such a backlog of accumulated emotional energy that we require increasing effort to keep it out of awareness. Addictions become necessary to stay one step ahead of this: alcohol and substance use, smoking cigarettes, working too much, obsessive thinking, overeating and under-eating, watching TV, and surfing the Internet all become methods of moving away from one's emotions, which continue to add up each day.

This strategy of turning our bodies off might actually have a chance if it weren't for intimate relationship. What works for us when we're by ourselves is thrown into chaos by trying to be close to another. Now someone wants us to be open and available, to talk about what is really going on, to "be there" when we're being physically intimate. Meanwhile, they're having all of their feelings. It's hard to be around a person who is having an emotional experience without feeling emotionally activated ourselves, especially if we haven't been tuning into and doing maintenance of our own internal state. Much of how we respond to someone else's emotional outbursts has to do with wishing that they'd stop having those big feelings. Trying to rush someone to feel better and trying to fix whatever is upsetting them by suggesting solutions are popular methods of encouraging them to get over whatever the emotion is.

What is it that is so difficult about actually feeling what is going on in our bodies? For many of us, just tuning into the roiling, unpredictable waves of energy is a frightening experience. Because this energy has been left unattended for so long, it often feels as though it has no end. Our sadness might seem like a bottomless well, our anger like a huge fuel plant about to explode, and our fear a relentless stalker ready to paralyze us. Because our encounters with our bodies tend to be so brief, when they do manage to get our attention, they usually have had to turn up the volume so high that all that energy feels way out of control. This is more fodder for our belief that emotions themselves are out of control, so they should stay out of awareness. This cycle winds more and more tightly, as we alternate between experiencing frightening intensity of emotion (which is our anxiety) and shutting down on ourselves entirely (the "depressing" part of our strategy). We might also experience ourselves as alternating between feeling triggered into reactivity (perhaps acting in impulsive and sometimes destructive ways) and then feeling deadened and shut down.

Mastering the art of experiencing and then shifting emotions is the path out of this life-strangling cycle. As you embark on this path, expect to feel somewhat unsettled for a while. If you haven't before been tuned in to the richness of your internal world, you might feel as if you have landed on a new planet. Know that this is the journey back to your real self, the essential *you* that can be found underneath all of these old, unfelt feelings.

Here's your map for this foreign land: What's stuck in your body is energy—energy that would naturally flow if you didn't dam it up. It was once anger, fear, sadness, gladness, or sexuality that you couldn't afford to feel, so you clenched down on it, stopping it in its tracks and clogging up your works. The whole function of emotion is to deliver data to you about how you are experiencing what is going on around you. That means that when it has communicated its message, emotion is designed to move on through, like any good messenger.

THE HOW-TO'S OF MOVING EMOTIONS

When we get overwhelmed by the intensity of an emotion—or if we decide it is invalid—we push it back down into our bodies. The task at hand is to locate the energy and help it move along its natural path out of the body. In this chapter, you'll learn how to clear the dam and support the flow.

Life-flow channel clearing is about moving emotions through and out of your body. This is a crucial part of getting unstuck, to actually un-stick your emotions. To move emotions, follow this sequence (which I'll go into below): notice the energy, accept it, allow it to become as big as it is, name it, ask it for its message, then breathe into it, appreciate it, and let it diffuse out of your body. As you get better and better at this process, you'll begin to notice how emotions move like waves through your body, gathering momentum, peaking into a crashing crescendo, and receding. At this point, you might feel like they are crashing over you and pulling you under, but soon you'll be like a surfer, riding with the energy waves and power.

The process of moving emotions is key to this work toward connecting with who you really are and showing your real self to others. Translating what your body is trying to tell you into words and then moving your emotions are what it takes to move out of projection and back into your essential self. I recommend you practice this process as much as you can: with yourself, your partner, and your friends; at stoplights; and while standing in line at the grocery store.

Give yourself time with this process and have patience—it will get easier! Mastering the sequence outlined below will give you an intimacy and sense of connection with your own experience that will deliver ongoing dividends to you. Try this standing up and while moving your body, since moving and breathing freely allow feelings to be more accessible. The list of steps looks long, but it will become much quicker and more flowing with some practice.

By the way, I'm aware that eight steps are a lot. Having worked with hundreds of people over the past twenty-five years, though, I recommend you give yourself the luxury of taking your time in walking through each of the steps listed below. Mastering the flow of this process is worth years of therapy, and may keep you out of divorce court. Having confidence in your ability to let emotion move through your body is the antidote to addictions, falling out of love, and disconnection from your loved ones. Letting your body be in flow will connect you to the flow of life, to your creativity, and to your beloved.

Moving Emotions Process

Step One: *Notice* your body from the top of your head to the tip of your toes. Note all the places that are trying to get your attention by being contracted, in pain, tense, tight, expanded, flowing, excited, light, agitated, hot, cold, or any other sensation.

Step Two: Choose one of these places to *focus* upon. Notice the quality of the energy and allow your attention to simply rest on it. This part is about simply tuning into sensation and *trying on the possibility that it is an expression of emotion* (versus the arguable, "I've always had a bad back—it's genetic" or "I know the queasiness in my stomach is from lunch").

Step Three: Once you've found the sensation, be present with it. Breathe into it. Let it be true, *accept* it. Have your internal voice give it permission to *be* (instead of what we often say inside, "There's nothing to be this upset about?"). This would sound like "hmmm, my chest feels tight and constricted [long in-breath]. It sure is tight." This is a crucial move into consciousness: validating the existence of your experience instead of making it wrong or pushing it away.

Step Four: Now let the energy *expand,* getting as big as it is. This can be the scary part for people. Most of us have the sense that were we to really let go, we'd go crazy, or explode, or become a puddle on the floor. But the energy needs to expand so it can move. Like those magic seahorses you can buy that start out as big as a dime and then grow to life-size when placed in water, this stuck energy will use your breath to expand back to its real size. Notice, however, that when you keep breathing into it, it will crescendo in its intensity and then start to loosen and move. Really, it will! (You may want to begin with a smaller sensation to experiment with to see if this is true.)

Step Five: While it's big, ask the energy to *label* itself *mad, sad, scared, glad, or sexual.* OK, this may sound strange. How is it supposed to know? But emotions are information, so if you get to know their different qualities, they will, indeed, be able to help you discern among them. As you get better at this, let yourself not be right. Try out each emotion like comparing a paint chip to a color, for example, "hmmm, yes, mostly scared with a little mad mixed in," or "yeah, this is pure sadness," or "sexual!"

Here are some tips in trying to figure this out. The "negative" emotions of anger, sadness, and fear got the reputation of being negative because they are made of dense and contracted energy. Anger tends to reside in the shoulders, neck, and head; sadness in the throat and chest; and fear in the belly, though we certainly mix and match them throughout our bodies. The more "positive" emotions of glad and sexual offer expanded sensations like movement, heat, and opening. We might feel them in specific areas (around the heart, in the genitals), but they also tend to feel like a larger expansion of the whole body.

Please note an important part of this step. I did *not* say: "Locate the sensation, decide what it is, and then figure out whether or not you have a good reason to feel this way. If you can't, push it away." That's how I learned to deal with my feelings, which took me straight into anxiety and depression. I learned to check outside of myself to decide whether there were valid reasons to be having the experience I was having. This is mind-in-charge: I should feel this. I shouldn't feel that. Instead, the powerful step toward moving emotion is to *let what is true, be true.* If the sensation is anger, let it be anger without judging it as appropriate or inappropriate. Same with all the others. It is sadness or fear or sexual feelings or gladness because, well, that's what it is. Most of us have some idea that it's okay to feel some feelings (maybe glad and sad), but not others (perhaps sexual, mad, and scared). This leaves our poor bodies trying their hardest to get our attention, signaling to us more and more loudly, but constantly being misunderstood. It's like a broadcast going out in English that is only interpreted in Swahili.

Step Six: So, you're experiencing your anger, fear, sadness, gladness, or sexual feelings, letting them be true. Good job! Now, see if you can *ask* what the message they're trying to deliver is. Ask the sensation itself: "What is my (mad/sad/scared/glad/sexual) trying to tell me?" This can be tricky, because usually our minds have all kinds of things to say about this. Things like, "I shouldn't be feeling angry because she didn't mean to do it," or "it's stupid to be scared; what's there to be scared about, really?" (Which takes us back to step five.) Ask your mind to step aside for a moment; this is between you and your body. As you are being with the sensation, an image or some words will probably float up. Try not to censor these, even if they don't make sense. If you can allow your inner experience to be true, it will *always* make sense. It might not be about today (you can also ask your emotions if they are from the past or the present), but given room and acceptance, your emotions will quite logically be attached to whatever triggered them.

> If you can allow your inner experience to be true,
> it will *always* make sense.

> If you can allow your inner experience to be true, it will *always* make sense.

When you get the answer to "What is my (mad/sad/scared/glad/sexual) emotion trying to tell me?" check it against the sensation to be sure it resonates as true. If it doesn't, keep asking the question until it does. Also check to make sure it is an answer that no one can argue with. Deciding, for example, that "I feel mad because he was mean to me" will keep everything stuck. On the other hand, "I feel mad and scared. I didn't like what he said, and I'm scared that I don't know how to take care of myself" will move things along. Notice that as this becomes clear, you are speaking the unarguable truth.

Step Seven: Now that they've delivered their message, you can *move* the feelings on their way. Focus back in on the original sensation (which may have already shifted by now to something else), appreciate it for its effort in telling you what is going on, and breathe into it. Just be with it with nonjudgmental attention and breath, until it passes through. It will.

Step Eight: *Celebrate* yourself and your body for communicating so well!

So, let's go through this again with an example. I'll walk you through my inner world of this moment.

1. *Notice:* I notice tightness in my upper back, chest, and jaw, and tiredness at the back of my eyes.

2. *Focus:* I focus on my upper back, since it is the most pronounced of sensations. It feels like it's in a vise.

3. *Accept:* Yep, it's true. My back is tight.

4. *Expand:* As soon as I put my attention on the tightness, I notice the energy expanding out to my sides and up my neck.

5. *Label:* Mad and scared.

6. *Ask:* I feel mad—it's about my wanting to push through obstacles and keep myself moving in this writing. I feel scared that I won't have enough time. Under that is fear that what I'm writing won't make sense; under that is fear that I won't be liked, and so I will be alone. What I want is to breathe and relax and enjoy this process.

7. *Move:* Actually, the tightness is mostly gone now. As I continue to simply pay attention to it, I notice it moving out of my body, leaving me with a warm and open sensation.

8. *Celebrate:* I'm sending energy of appreciation to my back, which I notice is increasing the sense of warmth.

TOOL   MOVING EMOTIONS PROCESS

Now you try going through these steps. This can be easier to do standing up, as moving and breathing allow us to fully access what is occurring in our body.

1. *Notice:* What are the sensations you notice?

2. *Focus:* The sensation that stands out the most is:

3. *Accept:* Breathe and allow yourself to just be with that sensation.

4. *Expand:* Let the sensation get bigger.

5. *Label:* Is it mad, sad, scared, glad, or sexual? Or is it a mixture? This sensation is:

6. *Ask:* What is the feeling trying to communicate to me? My emotions are telling me:

7. *Move:* Breathe into and pay attention to the sensation until it moves or shifts.

8. *Celebrate:* Take a moment to appreciate your body and its sensations for communicating to you so effectively.

Bringing It Back into Relationship

chapter 7

The Moving Emotions Process connects you to your real self. Could you feel that? There you are, in your body, allowing your experience to just be what it is, telling yourself the truth. If you're willing to ask and notice in a nonjudgmental way, your body is completely trustworthy in communicating to you what is really going on in there.

Intimacy happens when one person connects to the truth of her or his experience and speaks it to the other in an unarguable way. The S.E.W. process allows full connection to self, then full connection to the other, who can stay open while nondefensively listening. This allows the speaker to be seen and heard at her most elemental level, which is truly, at base, what most of us want in relationship. When the other person can do the same thing, the circuit is completed, and closeness and connection are ensured. Conflict drops away, empathy and a sense of alliance heighten, and new creative possibilities begin to appear. As both people master moving their emotions through easily, they will begin to notice the cue of contraction as a signal to stop and find out what is going on. Once the feelings are felt, understood, and spoken, it is possible to quickly move back into expansion and connection.

In my relationship, I used to complain, "We're not connected!" It wasn't until doing this process that I understood that I wasn't connected to *me*. Because I wasn't letting myself feel my sensations or link them to my emotions and what they were trying to communicate to me, there was no way I could be connected to my partner. I can still feel the huge relief of coming back home to my own body and of understanding how reliable and steadfast its messages were. It was like discovering a best friend that had been with me all along, through thick and thin.

In other words, the Moving Emotions Process is a core skill in creating intimacy. Before you begin to practice this with someone else, however, there is one other part to add. This is the skill of *openhearted listening*. For the circuit to completely connect, the listener has to really hear the speaker, with no filters. That is, the listener must be in his body, breathing, while hearing what the speaker is really trying to communicate. Often, we do other things (which are really about our internal defenses) such as

> » listening for blame;
> » planning our response or counterargument;
> » getting critical;
> » preparing to fix the problem;
> » getting triggered; and
> » using other defenses, such as spacing out, getting sleepy, thinking about the grocery list, and so on.

The body signals that cue you that you are in nonjudgmental, nonfiltering listening mode are: you're relaxed and breathing, you can track what your partner is saying, you are curious about her experience, and you are able to understand and summarize what she is telling you (even if you don't agree with it).

A surefire method for creating connection and intimacy is to communicate one's deepest experience in a way that can be heard by the other openly and nondefensively. That's what the next exercise is about, both to know and connect with one's own experience, and to be able to truly hear the other's experience.

TOOL   OPENHEARTED LISTENING CHECKLIST

For the next interaction you have with someone, have this checklist handy. Read it ahead of time, then again after the interaction. Which of the items below occurred? (Keep in mind that you're just noticing what happens without judgment about your skills.)

❏ I kept coming back to my breath, letting myself breathe deeply, while he talked.

❏ I let my body move.

❏ I noticed these filters:
   » criticism
   » seeing myself as better than or worse than
   » preparing my response while she talked
   » having a right-wrong mind-set
   » trying to figure out who is to blame
   » coming up with a solution without being asked
   » tuning out
   » other: _____

❏ I (was/was not) reactive. If I was reactive,
   » I stayed reactive for _____ (minutes/hours).
   » I found my way back to flow by _____

❏ I was able to be curious, asking open-ended questions.

❏ I understood the essence of what he was trying to communicate with me.

TOOL MOVING THROUGH EMOTIONS TOGETHER

Do this standing with a partner. Notice that the speaker only reads the questions and refrains from commenting about the feeler's experience, or from doing anything at all to "fix" the experience. (Having the Openhearted Listening Checklist available will help.)

(The speaker reads the list below to the feeler.)

1. *(Notice)* Scan through your body, noticing all the places in your body where you feel tension. Which one stands out the most?

2. *(Focus)* Let yourself focus in on that sensation. How would you describe the physical feelings?

3. *(Accept)* Let yourself just be present and notice what that particular sensation feels like in your body. Observe the sensation without judgment.

4. *(Expand)* Breathe into the sensation, allowing it to get as big as it is.

5. *(Label)* When you let yourself be aware of this physical sensation, without thinking about it or trying to make sense of it, does it feel mostly like *mad, sad, scared, glad,* or *sexual?*

6. *(Ask)* As you are breathing into it, begin to wonder what the emotion is trying to tell you. Let it not make any sense. (Note that the feeler may not know anything about it at all, which is fine.)

7. *(Move)* Now focus on moving the feeling through your body by breathing into it with nonjudgmental attention, and watching as it moves.

8. *(Celebrate!)* Take a moment to appreciate yourself and your body for communicating with you so well.

9. Switch roles.

ADVANCED TIPS
FOR EMOTIONAL MASTERY

chapter 8

Are you starting to get the hang of this emotional world? Notice that while it might seem like a foreign land, it actually is all very logical. Do you see how it works?

> » Something happens.
> » Our bodies generate a sensation (or sensations) to communicate our experience of that something.
> » We translate the sensation into one (or more) emotion(s).
> » We support the movement of the emotion through our body (by noticing it, focusing on it, accepting it, letting it get bigger, labeling the emotion, and asking it to communicate its information).
> » We tell the unarguable truth so that another can hear us nondefensively.
> » We end up with new information about ourselves and the world.

What an elegant system.

Now that you're getting the hang of tuning into your body and the wealth of information that it is constantly generating, here are some advanced tips about how emotions work.

» Notice how you can have your entire experience of your emotional world without *doing* anything. Many people have learned that having an emotion means acting on the emotion. This belief can make life pretty dicey when the emotion is mad or sexual. If mad or sexual feelings surge to the surface and we don't know that we can just let them flow through, it can seem like our choice is to act them out or to just shut them down. This can lead to shutting out our most powerful and life-enhancing sensations.

» The alternative is to simply tune in to these feelings and allow them to be as big as they are. Like being in the middle of a thunderstorm, it can be very useful to wait to act until the storm has fully passed through. At that point, sometimes you may choose an action; it is also possible to just be present and breathe, fully experiencing the body sensations that accompany these emotions.

» Remember: *you are the source.* It might seem like someone "made you" mad or scared or sexual. Nope. You are a trigger waiting to happen. All those times you didn't actually move your emotions through your body (from childhood to now) means that you have unprocessed emotions. When someone activates one of those old emotions, it means it can finally move through. Instead of blaming that person, you might want to thank him or her.

» *Anyone gets to feel anything, anytime, for any reason.* Right? Just checking.

» While being full of information, emotions don't actually mean much. They're actually just a physiological and chemical event that is moving through our body until they get metabolized. When we're in their grip, we may want to do something drastic: End the relationship! Quit the job! Say the mean thing. Fake our own deaths and start a new life. Truly, waiting for an emotion to just pass through (kind of like a bad case of gas) can allow our minds to clear so we can choose an action (that isn't just a *re-action*).

My Feelings Have Nothing to Do with You

One of the greatest challenges of relationship comes from a natural aspect of our most basic humanness: *emotions are contagious.*

Does this sound familiar?

Patricia: "I've had a terrible day. My boss is such a jerk."

George: "What happened this time?"

Patricia: "I gave her that report that she wanted, and all she did was tear it apart."

George: "Did you stand up to her like we talked about?"

Patricia: "I tried, but she wouldn't hear anything I said."

George: "But did you tell her what you think?"

Patricia: "She just won't hear it."

George: "Or maybe you need to do a better job."

Patricia: "Whose side are you on?"

George: "Oh great. Here we go. I'm just trying to help."

Patricia: "Why can't you just listen to me? Why do you have to try to fix me?"

George: "Fine. Go ahead and be miserable."

Patricia: "I just want to have my feelings."

George: "Yeah, right [picking up his iPad]. I've got some work to do."

For the most part, physiological systems in the human body are closed loops. Blood circulates through one person's body, not the other's. Spinal fluid is contained within one body. Digestion, hormones, and metabolism, these are all personal processes that we don't share with anyone else.

Then we come to emotions. Emotions are designed to be shared. Their function is to create instant chemical communication, both to ourselves about our own experience of the world as well as to those around us. Our posture, facial expression, voice tone, breath rate and depth, and muscle clenching or relaxation are all instant cues as to our emotional state, both internally and externally.

The open-loop nature of our emotional system means that others are impacted by our state and we are impacted by theirs, creating a resonance chamber that pings signals back and forth. The brain's mirror neurons mean that watching and listening to you will create your emotional experience in my body.

This built-in emotional reproduction ability leads to tremendous advantages. Parents can tune in to what their children are experiencing and needing. Kids feel a natural affinity and compassion for each other that turns into helping behaviors, emotional connection, and friendship. Partners can often intuit each other's emotional states instantly.

However, there's a whole other aspect to our empathic abilities that is at the heart of most relationship challenges. When people we care about have emotions, we seem to feel compelled to help them feel better. That makes sense, doesn't it? When those around us are distressed, we feel distressed. When they feel better, we feel better. Unfortunately, while our wanting our loved one to not be distressed might be well intentioned, as soon as we swing into action to help, we jump into the eddy of emotional entanglement.

Here's one version of how this looks: You feel upset. I try to help soothe you. You think I think there's something wrong with how you're feeling. So you feel more upset. So I try to help and fix more, until we're in a tug-of-war about your emotional experience. If this continues, you ultimately have to get away from me to actually take care of yourself to feel better.

Does that dance seem familiar? How about this one? I'm reactive, so you offer me suggestions. I halfheartedly try your ideas (because they weren't mine). You perceive my wimpy efforts to change as being signs of some sort of character defect ("She never follows through on what she says she's going to do."). Now you're irritated with me, so I try to placate you by trying harder to please you until I give up and don't try at all. Then, in our frustration with me, we both decide there is really something wrong with me.

There are other flavors of emotional entanglements, but they all come back to the same origin: people get confused about how to be emotionally supportive, defaulting to trying to fix and control emotional distress through intellectual solution. Suddenly partners are fighting about the arguable, instead of focusing on moving their emotions.

This sticky minefield needs a good list of tips, don't you think? Here they are—these are worth keeping handy.

Tips for Responding When Someone You Love Has an Emotion

(Which, if your partner is breathing, is all the time.)

1. *Your only job is to keep breathing.* While there is a common belief that being a good and caring partner means trying to get into the emotional ring with your loved one, I see that as a slippery slope into entanglement. Instead, I suggest you let her have her own experience. You'll be impacted by what she is feeling, so let yourself focus on your own body, moving whatever you're feeling through with attention and breath.

2. Remind yourself that *anyone gets to feel anything, anytime, for any reason.*

3. Remind yourself that *your partner's feelings have nothing to do with you.* We're each the source of our own experience, remember? So even if you did forget his birthday or sound exactly like his mother when you asked him how he spent that money, whatever chain of emotions that triggered in your partner is his to have. Give your partner space to have it.

4. *Meanwhile, it's your job to have your own emotions.* Your emotions have nothing to do with your partner.

5. *Ask if your partner wants you to help solve the problem.* Sometimes you'll get a yes; often you won't. It's good manners to ask if someone wants your help before imposing it on him.

6. *Ask if your partner wants your psychological interpretations.* I trained for years in psychological

assessment and interpretation of human behavior, and I'm still cautious about offering my ideas about someone's unconscious motivation. Yet partners seem to feel comfortable tossing around comments like, "I think you're only doing this to please your father," or "You clearly have issues around addiction." You may, indeed, have the closest, clearest view of your partner's inner workings, but you also may have a little bit of an objectivity problem. Plus, there's that rudeness issue.

7. *You get to decide whether you're available to provide emotional support.* Just because you're in an intimate relationship doesn't mean you're supposed to be available anytime, anywhere. You get to say, "I'm not able to be present with you right now."

8. *Know there's a difference between complaining and having emotions.* People need to vent, which usually means they're not ready to solve the issue. You can ask them what they really want. (However, I do view venting and complaining as being the equivalent of emotionally vomiting. Afterward, the complainer usually feels better, while the listener might feel toxified. Try the Conscious Complaining exercise on page 86 to deal with this.)

9. *Sometimes what is most helpful is basic physical soothing.* I think talking is overrated. When people are upset, our systems mostly just need to calm down. Taking your partner's hand, sitting next to each other on the couch with your legs touching, just hugging or holding each other can be much more effective than talking about the problem.

Extra Note to Fixers

For those of you who learned the idea that to be a good partner, you're supposed to be able to fix whatever your loved one is experiencing, here are some special instructions. Usually fixing looks like offering solutions or trying to "make her feel better," which generally means trying to get her to stop feeling those "bad" feelings. What that really does is completely stop any progression through the process, getting things stuck.

So, if you want to be helpful, here's how to do that: *help her move feelings.* Mostly that means getting out of the way of her process, allowing her to have her experience on her own timing. If *invited,* however, the two of you can be allies in this process, and you can say things to facilitate this movement. Here are some things you can say along the way (again, *if invited*):

> What are you feeling?
> Where is it in your body?
> What does that feel like?
> Does it remind you of anything?
> That makes sense.
> I understand.
> Tell me more.
> What are you feeling now?
> What do you really want?

Lots of head-nodding and compassionate "umm-hmms" also will help. Then, try to get out of the way so she can have her experience.

You'll know you're on your way toward mastering emotions when you notice an increasing level of aliveness and vitality. Relating to whatever is happening in your body with loving detachment, noticing it, allowing it to be true, and then letting it pass through is a path to a bigger life. You'll start to see how letting your inner emotional storms move will clear out old emotional clutter, making space for more expansion, bigger energy, and deeper intimacy. Eventually, you will enjoy the flow of your own experience while simultaneously contacting your essential self, the deep serenity touched by the power of emotional communication.

EMOTIONAL FLOW: BLOCKS AND UNBLOCKING

chapter 9

The art of creating a passionate, connected, alive relationship relies on keeping emotional flow going. Rivers can move through the landscape, their waters coursing, rushing, and flowing with life. Alternatively, they can get dammed up into stagnation and sluggishness. Much of what you've learned up to now is about removing the dam, letting the flow clear out what was blocking connection and passion. In this chapter, you'll learn how you are blocking yourself and how to remove the obstacles to flow.

Block One: Getting Hijacked by Reactive Brain

Imagine you're out driving, listening to some great music, humming along, feeling relaxed. Suddenly a car pulls out in front of you, and you stomp on the brakes. Do you cuss and yell and give the driver the finger? Do you feel paralyzed? Do you just sit listening to your heart pounding in your ears?

All mammals have Reactive Brain, the part of the brain that reacts instantly, automatically, without any thought. Reactive

Brain is what enabled you to survive to read this workbook; if you didn't have a Reactive Brain, the bus would have run you over, or you wouldn't have gotten out of the way of the falling rock. That instant mechanism is a great design for survival but a real troublemaker in relationship.

Reactive Brain triggers fleeing, fighting, and freezing. Our survival as a species has depended on a lightning-quick response to external threat. We had to be able to flee the lion, turn and face the attacking warrior, or freeze in the grass until the predator passed by. There are few of these actual threats to life and limb these days, but our bodies are still programmed for them. And relationship can bring up something that can seem equally frightening to physical threat: a threat to the sense of who we are.

Conflict can trigger us into the fight-flight-freeze response. There may be a slow progression into this, or it may occur very quickly, but our whole physiology changes as we consciously or unconsciously perceive ourselves to be threatened. Our pulse quickens, our blood pressure rises, and our muscles tighten, as our whole body prepares to meet the threat.

It would be so helpful if something about us physically changed when we go into Reactive Brain. The Incredible Hulk had the advantage of those around him knowing when he was triggered into anger. Unfortunately, we typically look pretty much the same before the instant we are triggered and after. Our partners have no idea that anything is different about us, yet our internal state has completely changed. Whereas in Creative Brain we can utilize the most advanced part of our brains, problem solving and sorting through an issue, now the blood is mostly being shunted to those parts that are most primitive and animal-like. Our most basic physiology takes over, and we are ready to *fight* or *get away* or *freeze* until the danger has passed. Unless there is some way to communicate this quickly and effectively, our partners are bound to want to continue to keep talking and problem solving (as they were that moment before). However, *there is no way for us to do this.* Reactive Brain cannot process efficiently and will not be able to until it is no longer triggered.

I want to repeat that. This part is really important. *Reactive Brain can't do anything else but react.*

Most conflicts escalate at this point. One person is triggered into the fight-flight-freeze response. The other person doesn't know this and wants to keep talking, often pressuring the first to continue. The triggered person gets increasingly reactive as his arousal level increases, further magnifying the perception of threat. By now, he's probably said something that seems threatening to the previously calm partner. As both go into fight-flight-freeze, neither has the ability to access Creative Brain, the part of the brain that can actually solve the issue. Often one person tries to leave (flee), which threatens the other even more. This is typically the point at which domestic violence happens, when one tries to leave and the other attempts to stop her.

Research by psychologist John Gottman illustrates how Reactive Brain can hijack a couple's interactions—and how shifting back to Creative Brain reconnects them to their own ability to solve their issues. (In fact, my whole approach to doing relationship work shifted when I read this research.) Gottman hooked partners up to physiological gauges and videotaped them while they discussed difficult issues. He and his researchers waited until each person's pulse was over one hundred beats per minute and then interrupted the argument, telling the couple that the camera had broken down. They instructed the couple to sit quietly and read magazines. Fifteen minutes later, they told the couple to begin again, saying that the equipment was fixed. (Actually, it was never broken.) What the researchers found was that once they had the time to get out of the high level of arousal, the couple was able to discuss the issue and problem solve it effectively, as if they were entirely different people.[9]

What I've taken from Gottman's brilliant research is that most people are able to solve their issues quite effectively, so long as they are not triggered into Reactive Brain. In fact, I believe I wouldn't have much of a career dealing with relationship issues if it weren't for Reactive Brain. When in Creative Brain, most of us have the ability to figure our lives out quite well. It's just that little problem of humans being hijacked by Reactive Brain but having no clue that their best selves are no longer in charge.

What's the trick to dealing with the escalation and deterioration of communication that Reactive Brain brings with it?

> Know that you or your partner *will get triggered*
> and have a strategy for this.

Know that you or your partner *will get triggered* and have a strategy for this.

This cannot be overemphasized. Without a strategy, couples are likely to get into a pattern of very toxic interactions, where they say or do the kind of things that they would never say or do otherwise. Even though, as individuals, we might believe these behaviors to be uncharacteristic of us, our partners see them as our hidden aspects that are apt to come out and attack them, as if they are our real selves. Over time, the relationship can take on a very negative tone, with these toxic interactions using up large amounts of the positive emotional reservoir accumulated during nonconflict times.

What the triggered body needs is (1) for the threat to stop, so it can (2) move out of its aroused state (which typically takes at least fifteen to twenty minutes, the time it takes for adrenaline to be metabolized). It needs a time-out from the interaction. Thus, the couple must have an agreement about how to stop an interaction immediately upon one of them becoming triggered. As straightforward as this sounds, it tends to be quite challenging for couples, particularly if one or both of them come from backgrounds where there was a great deal of fighting. (Often, this occurred in the family context of sibling fighting. If you want to trace your pattern of fighting, look at how you interacted with your brothers and sisters as well as with your parents.) The goal is to stop the momentum of the runaway horse before it has trampled the relationship. Of course, this is much easier to do before the horse begins to break out in a run, that is, as the pulse is quickening, before one's physiology is completely triggered.

> If your pulse is faster than one hundred
> beats per minute, stop *talking!*[10]

When you are making a time-out agreement together (see page 78), understand that as with any good agreement, both of your needs must be addressed. The triggered person must know the interaction will stop immediately; the nontriggered person must know when the triggered person will return and that the issue will get dealt with at some point.

> It takes fifteen to twenty minutes
> for adrenaline to be metabolized.[11]

Block Two: Avoiding Emotions (Drifts)

Imagine that you and your partner are heading out of town. You're feeling good and excited about having an adventure. On the way out the door, you see the overgrown grass in the front yard. Your stomach clutches, but you don't tune into that sensation. Instead, the following exchange takes place:

Person One: "I thought you said you'd mow the yard."

Person Two: "I've been really busy."

One: "You're always busy. I just can't count on you to do what you say you'll do."

Two: "Look, I try as hard as I can. I can't do *everything.* You expect too much of me."

If your pulse is faster than one hundred beats per minute, *stop talking!*

It takes fifteen to twenty minutes for adrenaline to be metabolized.

TOOL TIME-OUT WORKSHEET

Take the time to fill out this worksheet when you both feel calm and relaxed. Practice time-outs ahead of time, like doing a fire drill together.

1. Each person answers by filling in the blank in this statement: When I get triggered into the fight-flight-freeze response, I typically need _____ (minutes/hours) to relax back into my regular state.

2. With #1 in mind, how long will your time-out last? Our time-outs will last: _____

3. Now make another agreement about how you will call a time-out. (For example, "Either of us can call a time-out at any time. When we do, we will stop immediately and take a breather for twenty minutes. We will then come back together. We'll then decide at what point in time we will try to resolve the issue.")

   We will call a time-out by:

4. Build into your agreement the difference between calling a time-out from all connection and a time-out from discussing a particular issue.

5. Recheck the agreement. Can you both fully stand behind it? Write the agreement in your journal.

6. List the activities you will do during the time-out to de-escalate and relax.

One: "Oh great. Here we go. I really wanted to have a good time on this trip, and now you're being like this."

Two: "Me! What about you?"

This exchange is a great demonstration of what Katie Hendricks calls a "drift."[12] We drift when something happens that triggers Reactive Brain and produces feelings we don't want to feel, leading to an interruption in ease, flow, and aliveness. And, in life something *always* happens. There's always going to be another traffic jam, another flat tire, an unexpected bill, or a loved one's illness and death. It is these unexpected occurrences that make life a never-ending adventure. And we humans, being quite fond of the illusion of control, tend to object to how our emotions rise up and tackle us out of nowhere. So we drift. We veer into long-term patterns of not feeling, of doing anything *but* feeling.

What prompts a drift—someone criticizing us, hearing a frightening story, having a deadline, the car making a strange sound—is less important than *noticing* that we're drifting. So, I'd like you to start to notice your very own favorite drifts (this tool is on page 80).

Unblocking through Shifts

Reactive Brain and drifts are the main blocks to having connected, passionate relationships and are, in large part, why relationships end. Couples either can't resolve conflict because of their reactivity, or they end up falling out of love because they've shut themselves down from what supports love and connection: emotional flow.

It's a simple idea, really: the path beyond these two relationship killers is to find a way to shift your body out of Reactive Brain and back into Creative Brain. Reactive Brain zips us into narrow focus, to what is wrong, to the threat. Creative Brain

TOOL LABELING YOUR DRIFTS

(Adapted from the "Drift & Shift" exercise[13] by Kathlyn Hendricks, PhD)

You are in a *drift* anytime you're not in flow, that is, feeling your feelings fully or feeling relaxed and happy in your body. Below is a list of possible drifts. Circle those that you recognize in yourself, adding any others you can think of.

My Favorite Drifts

Blaming	Helping	Controlling
Criticizing	Compulsive exercise	Directing
Defending	Self-loathing	Distancing
Using substances	Making jokes	Ruminating
Spacing out	Judging	Complaining
Attacking	Collapsing	Surfing the Internet
Getting sleepy	Going invisible	Other:
Withdrawing	Reading	
Watching TV	Fixing	

finds its way to open focus, to possibilities, and to the other as ally.[14] Over and over, the work of relationship is to notice when we're in Reactive Brain, choose to shift, and then problem solve and connect from Creative Brain.

As you read through and practice the shifts below, notice what is missing: verbal processing. None of what I'm suggesting here says: "Talk about the issue until you resolve it. No matter how long it takes." (Many couples seem to think that longer is better. I think the record might go to one couple that "processed" an issue for ten hours straight. Unfortunately, the issue didn't get resolved. All that happened was that they used up their relationship's well-being bank account.) In fact, I'd strongly suggest the opposite. If you find yourself in Reactive Brain or in the middle of one of your favorite drifts, *do not try to process or solve the issue.*

Your brain can't do it. (As with much of what I teach, I learned this the hard way. I notice that once I'm in Reactive Brain, my mind starts telling me all kinds of unhelpful things, all of which reflect my escalated state. In my commitment to create a relationship of ease and flow with my partner, I've learned to not listen to what my Reactive Brain is telling me, unless, of course, the house really is on fire.)

> If you haven't solved an issue in fifteen minutes,
> stop talking! Do something, anything else.
> Come back to the issue when you're in Creative Brain.

Instead of sitting around trying to talk about the issue, all of the shifts listed below focus on changing what is happening in your body. Change your body, and you'll make your way back to Creative Brain, where you'll discover new resources you couldn't otherwise access. Having a repertoire of ways to shift gives you many choices at any given moment, so that you can move back to feeling really good.

Following are some recommended ways to shift out of Reactive Brain and drifts, and back into Creative Brain.

If you haven't solved an issue in fifteen minutes, stop talking! Do something, anything else. Come back to the issue when you're in Creative Brain.

Breathe

Remembering to breathe deeply is a simple, tried-and-true way to shift out of Reactive Brain back into the ease and flow of Creative Brain. The fight-flight-freeze response of Reactive Brain relies on fast, shallow breathing. Interrupting this automatic response with slow, deep breaths will immediately begin to change the brain's physiology. If you've been numbing out with drifts, breathing will take you back into direct contact with your inner world.

Move

When we're triggered into Reactive Brain, our bodies are preparing to fight (fists clenched, muscles pumped) or flee (legs and arms activated) or freeze (muscles frozen to "play dead"). Doing something—anything—to consciously change these automatic reactions will pull us out of the clutches of Reactive Brain. Fighters can unclench; fleers can run around or jump up and down; freezers can surreptitiously wiggle their toes. And if you've been drifting, you will remember that you actually have a body.

Say Something Unarguable

I did say to avoid verbal processing. But I don't mean don't talk. Tuning into your sensations will bring you out of reactivity and drifts, and back to your body. Describing them to someone else will clue them into your inner world. Labeling your emotions will get you out of the spin of Reactive Brain and remind you that you have emotions. Uncovering what you really want will bring you back into contact with you and support forward movement out of stuckness.

Be Curious; Wonder

Reactive Brain wants to be right. It loves the illusion of a controlled and predictable world (as defined by its view of reality). Just using words like *I'm curious* and *I wonder* breaks the trance of Reactive Brain.

Do the Moving Emotions Process

Remember this? It's in chapter 6. Reactive Brain wants to stay stuck; drifts want to keep drifting. Following the Moving Emotions Process will return you to flow.

Appreciate: Yourself, Someone Else, Anything at All

Choosing to appreciate something for no good reason at all (as Gay Hendricks advises) creates an immediate shift.[15] While the job of Reactive Brain is to figure out what is wrong (notice that once you find one wrong thing, it leads to an endless chain), getting your brain to find out what is right puts it right on the path to Creative Brain. (I have appreciated many unusual items, including asphalt and stoplights. It all works.)

Laugh

Did you know you can start laughing just because you decide to? Yep, you're the source of laughing, too! While it can be provocative to start laughing in the middle of a conflict, it also makes what seems so deadly serious become as absurd as it really is.

Play

Creative expression of any sort will interrupt the ruts of Reactive Brain and drifting. The point of reaction is that it's not new. It's the same old, same old, the well-worn track that the brain wants to automatically follow. Doing something—anything—different pops you out of the track. Whistling, wagging your tail, growling, dancing, singing your complaint in operatic tones, using finger puppets, arguing while bent upside down, making paper airplanes and flying them around, running around the block, jumping to drumming music, anything different will be different.

Touch

Touch soothes mammals. Not always, for sure—some people don't welcome touch when they're upset. But simple physical connection is a way to move beyond the words, beyond the beliefs and all the trouble that the mind can start. Shifting out of the fight-flight-freeze mode of Reactive Brain means reminding the body that there isn't a real threat. Touching hands lightly and sitting with legs or arms brushing together allows people to calm down and remember that they are actually allies, not enemies.

Eye Contact

Along with touch, coming into eye contact with each other can be challenging in the throes of conflict. If you let yourself look into each other's eyes, though, you'll instantly initiate a physiological shift back into connection. And there is nothing like having to really look at the other person to interrupt a drift.

Special Note: Unblocking Sexual Flow

Remember how sexuality is part of life energy? That means it is subject to the same blocks and drifts that stop all of the other emotions. And that potentially sets up big issues for couples.

When Reactive Brain takes over, sexual feelings often (though not always) go underground. Anger, fear, and sadness generally need attention to be moved through before a person is able to feel the more expanded emotions of glad and sexual. Taking the time to speak the unarguable truth and then move emotions through can reconnect partners and reignite passion.

Power struggles are often the main culprit in sexual issues. We'll get to how to unwind those struggles in part 3. The bottom line in keeping passion strong and the fires hot is to use the same skills that you've already been learning: Speak the (unarguable) truth. Feel your feelings. And say what you really want.

TOOL   CREATING A SHIFT REPERTOIRE

(Adapted from the "Drift & Shift" exercise[16] by Kathlyn Hendricks, PhD)

Read through the list of shifts on pages 82–84. Try them out in your body. Which ones do you want to use when you go into Reactive Brain and drifts? Write these down in your journal and commit to using them.

My Favorite Shifts and How I'll Use Them:

New Shifts I'd Like To Try Out:

TOOL   COMMITTING TO SHIFTING

As you think about your daily schedule, what additional shifting activities would you like to incorporate into your life? What supports you in living in a more expanded way?

In your journal, note the ongoing shifting and expanding activities that you commit to incorporating into your daily schedule.

TOOL   CONSCIOUS COMPLAINING

Sometimes people just aren't ready to communicate in a conscious way.
Use these steps whenever one of you wants to complain, vent, or blame.

1. The complainer requests two to five minutes of the listener's time.

2. The listener agrees and prepares by breathing, noticing body signals,
   and letting her body move around.

3. The complainer complains *full out!* Gestures, dramatic expression and tone,
   and big movements are all welcomed and encouraged by the listener.

4. After the allotted time, go do something fun!

RELATIONSHIP AS EMOTIONAL HEALER

chapter 10

I want to revisit the powerful idea that *what we are triggered by can heal us.*

What I notice with couples that are having trouble is that they think they know what the problem is. ("He never listens to me." "She never wants to be intimate." "I'm just not in love.") They don't notice the real culprit: Reactive Brain. This oversight seems based in the belief that they should never be triggered. The logical (but misinformed) strategy becomes to spend time and energy trying to train their partner to not trigger them. Do any of these statements sound familiar?

"Please don't use that tone with me."

"I wish you would just give me some time to transition when I walk through the door."

"You're such a downer. Can't you cheer up? I would feel better."

"Why are you always so upbeat? I think you must be bipolar."

"This was supposed to be a romantic evening. Now you've ruined it!"

"You're just like my (father/mother/sister/brother/perpetrator/ex)."

"If you would just stop (fill in the blank), I would be able to be more (vulnerable/comfortable/open/sexual/emotional/fill in the blank)."

> The real problem for humans is that we are threatened animals who can speak.

With the idea that Reactive Brain is to be avoided at all costs, partners end up with lists of things they're supposed to do or not do in order to keep the other person from being triggered. (I know this from trying—and failing—to train myself and my partner to follow our lists. I ultimately realized that when I was triggered, I couldn't even remember what was on my own list, let alone what I was supposed to do for her.)

If the goal is to stay out of Reactive Brain, when someone is triggered, it becomes a signal that someone failed. In other words, *the couple's efforts to do the right thing shut off the very flow that allows for passion and authenticity.*

Reactive Brain is part and parcel of being human. It's part of how our brain functions, remember?

Let's take a moment to appreciate Reactive Brain, and to forgive ourselves—and each other—for having one.

Sure, we think and say awful things when we're in Reactive Brain. So do our partners. We act like the threatened mammals that we experience ourselves to be. The trigger gets pulled, and we yell or collapse or imagine homicide or suicide or just getting the hell out of there. Oh well. That's how our species managed to survive until now, by reacting automatically and immediately to threat.

The real problem for humans is that we are threatened animals who can speak.

Poor Reactive Brain. It's doing the best it can.

The plot thickens when you imagine all the times in your life when you went into Reactive Brain but didn't fully process what happened. That emotional energy piles up and comes back to haunt you.

If you imagine all the feelings you haven't felt and moved through you since birth, you can see how there could be hundreds, maybe thousands of layers of energy that have accumulated in your body. *It is these layers of energy that get triggered.* Yes, you're walking around, just waiting to be triggered into old feelings. Now, thanks to your partner, the triggers are inevitable. It is the gift of intimacy. Whereas, with less intense relationships, we can behave pretty consistently and mostly in a fairly civilized way, close relationships seem to provide the perfect medium within which the old, unfelt feelings will arise, and with them, old behaviors.

This can be a magnificent setup for healing if the experience of being triggered is one of feeling old feelings and letting them pass through the body. Generally, however, an old emotion gets provoked and we take it seriously, believing that we're viewing reality accurately. For example, if our partner comes in late and we get triggered into anger and fear, we usually justify our experience. Anyone would get angry at that thoughtlessness, right? Were we to pull the feelings apart, however, we might find a far more interesting picture. Here's a possible scenario, were we to look under the surface at our body's experience.

1. What are the sensations? *My heart is pounding, my jaw is tight, and I have tightness in my chest.*

2. What feelings go with this? *Mad and scared.*

3. How much of this feels old (that is, not about this incident)? *Most of it.*

4. What are the bottom lines about my fear? *I'm afraid I'm not important. I was afraid something happened to my partner that made him late. I'm afraid that I have no control.*

5. What are the bottom lines about my anger?
I feel mad that I don't have the control that I want.

6. What does this remind me of about being a kid?
Feeling scared I wasn't important in my family.
Not having control over time.

Noticing how today's issue is bringing up yesterday's feelings allows us to move those old feelings through our body, fully experiencing them (as we couldn't when we first had them) and then releasing them.

I love the simplicity and elegance of this process and follow it in sessions with my clients. (This is a reason I enjoy doing couples' work so much—the built-in triggers are sitting next to each other. Though I have to admit that I'm not usually jumping for joy when I'm the one who is triggered.)

The alternative to consciously riding the flow of triggered emotions to completion is to stay unconscious about all of this. We then can enlist our partner as our co-star in the reenactments of all of these old issues. If we are unwilling to feel what is still in our bodies, when these emotions get triggered we'll just project them, blaming our partners. The irony here is that *we cannot allow our partners to change what we're blaming them for.* If they did, we'd have to finally feel what we've been avoiding. We end up placing them in a total bind: we get mad at them for triggering us, but we need them to keep triggering us so we can finally feel these stuck emotions.

The solution to this bind lies in each person's willingness to see herself as the source of whatever she is feeling, and to take responsibility for feeling it and moving it through her body.

(Remember the idea that you're the source?) This means under-standing that *every blame is a projection*. Yes, not only that, but so are *all judgments and criticisms*. Yep, these are all projections.

You might want to breathe with this idea, because it's quite different from how most of our culture operates. Much media content and many party conversations center on blame, judg-ment, and projection. Giving up that pastime could make you stand out from the crowd. But taking responsibility instead of blaming and projecting is a necessary step to finding our true power and creating the reality in which we live. It's the differ-ence between experiencing reality as happening to us (and so seeing ourselves as victims of our lives) and seeing how actively we are participating in creating our life circumstances.

This is a big subject that takes us to the next part of this book.

THE ROUTE TO
TRUE POWER

part three

No one is more powerful than when
living from one's true essence.

Taking Healthy Responsibility

chapter 11

100% Responsibility = 100% Power

Conflict and power struggles thrive on blame. It is an endless search, the pursuit of all the ways in which the other person was wrong (mean, hurtful, insensitive, etc.), with the accompanying pressure on him to change and the ensuing tangle into conflict.

These conflicts would instantly end with this simple, powerful move:

> Each person takes total responsibility for creating the problem and looks at how to change whatever it is he or she did.

100% Responsibility = 100% Power

Used here, responsibility is not about who is to blame ("Who is responsible for this?!"). It is a shift away from assigning the "wrong" position and toward the empowerment that comes from facing one's own behavior without defense. Can you imagine? Suddenly relationship offers the profound gift of offering instant feedback about who we are and the impact of our behavior, letting us notice and then alter those aspects of ourselves that just don't work very well. Our partners, then, would be our allies who could offer support for us to look at ourselves curiously, with an eye toward being as powerful as possible.

Taking responsibility in relationship is about moving out of defensiveness into a willingness to learn what we can from every interaction.[17] It is about being truly *able to respond* effectively to our life circumstances.

Embodying the concept of taking healthy responsibility over time has created some of the most powerful shifts that have occurred in my own relationship. Having once been a champion blamer, I discovered that simply choosing to take responsibility in the moment allows my body to relax and my mind to discover new possibilities, which is so much more fun than trying to see who or what is wrong.

Here's an example of how this shift into responsibility and out of blame can look.

John and Michael live together and have a shared bank account. They are fighting because John overdrew the account again. In the first interaction, clearly each perceives himself to be the victim of the other. The goal in this very typical struggle is to rack up blaming points, which will ultimately determine who is the winner and who is the loser.

> Each person takes total responsibility for creating the problem and looks at how to change whatever it is he or she did.

Michael: "I just looked at our account and saw that you bounced three checks. I can't believe you did this again!"

John: "Yeah, I'm sorry."

Michael: "That's what you said the last time. You told me you weren't going to let this happen again."

John: "Well, I tried. I just lost track."

Michael: "Why are you always so irresponsible! I can't believe what a child you are!"

John: "If you weren't always on my back, just waiting
for me to mess up, maybe I could get somewhere.
You are so controlling!"

Michael: "Someone has to be in control of this mess."

John: "Oh, right, like you know everything."

Michael: "I sure know more than you."

John: "You know, I'm really getting sick of this.
I need some space."

Michael: "Fine! Why don't you just go, the way you
always do when the chips are down?"

John: "I can't believe what a jerk you can be.
Whatever happened to the Michael I fell in
love with?"

Clearly, this conversation isn't going anywhere good. (Notice
the signs that each is in Reactive Brain. A time-out would
really help here.) The problem with this win-lose setup is
that people rarely volunteer for the loser position, so typically they won't go down without a big fight. Further, even if
one person were the clear winner, why would he want to be
intimate with a loser?

Let's switch to a different scenario, where each is willing to
take responsibility.

John: "I want to let you know that I bounced three
checks today."

Michael: "Oh. My whole body just contracted.
I feel scared and angry."

John: "Yeah, it's hard for me to breathe. I feel afraid that you're angry. Really, though, I'm more afraid that I'm not tracking my check writing."

Michael: "I'm afraid of being out of control. I think this is reminding me of being a kid, when my parents fought about money all the time. I can see how I've started acting like my mother when she was trying to control my father's spending."

John: "I think I rely on you to do that sometimes. As long as you're watching our money, I guess I feel better, like there's someone taking care of me."

Michael: "That makes sense."

John: "What if we sit down later, when we've both had time to chill out, and come up with a new way to handle money together?"

Michael: "That sounds great."

Of these two conversations, which one do you think will lead to actual change in the relationship? Which one promotes intimacy?

What John and Michael did in the second conversation might sound complicated and difficult, but it isn't. They used some skills, all of which promote taking total responsibility. I'll go over these now. (Some of these will probably sound familiar.)

1. They spoke the unarguable truth: each referenced what was going on in his body, starting with himself as the source. (In the first conversation, each was focused on what the other was doing to make his life difficult. This results in putting a lot of energy

into what we have zero control over: changing the other person.)

2. Neither tried to "fix" the other's experience. Feelings were spoken and given space to be true.

3. Because of the overall nondefensive tone of the conversation, each was able to become curious about what was going on under the surface. *It is these unconscious patterns that are driving the interaction;* uncovering them is the first step to changing the *real* problem.

4. Overall, John and Michael were able to remain allies with each other, working together to unearth what each was doing to create the issue.

5. They decided not to try to solve the issue while in the grip of Reactive Brain and will create some new agreements about money later. (A wonderful skill that I'll get to in chapter 14.)

Moving out of blame and into responsibility allows for a monumental shift out of struggle and into possibility. It is a powerful antidote to the depression and bitterness that result from seeing oneself as powerless, a victim of circumstances. Taking this step magically transforms the stuck muckiness of power struggle into a flowing rushing river of creative energy. (That's the miraculous shift that I felt when I was sitting across from my partner on the floor, so completely stuck, so many years ago.)

A major misperception that keeps people from stepping into responsibility is that this means that the blame shifts from the other to the self. That is, if it isn't your fault, it's my fault. Or maybe it's someone else's fault. Of course, the object of pinpointing who is at fault is to discover who is the bad one. It's a game of toxic hot potato, tossing around the energy of shame. ("You're bad!" "No I'm not, you're bad!" "Oh, OK, I really am bad. In fact, I'm such a piece of crap, I'm going to go punish myself.") This dynamic takes the neutral energy of relationship and perverts it into destructiveness, pulling each person into a swirling abyss of misery.

Choosing to take responsibility is about moving away from blame entirely. Whether I blame you or me or the weather or the president makes no difference: to blame is to give or drain away personal power. *Anytime we blame, we are giving away our power.* Refusing to blame, that is, taking full responsibility in any interaction, is our quickest route back into empowerment. Complaining is just another form of blaming and so, giving away power. If you watch yourself (or listen to others), you can literally feel the energy draining out of your body as you or they complain. It's the energetic equivalent of flushing money down the drain. There might be a moment of adrenaline peak that comes from the drama, but in the end, the money is still gone forever.

Stepping into taking responsibility is different from apologizing. Often apologizing becomes a placeholder, a way to not actually deal with the issue at all. The quick "I'm really sorry I'm late" or off-handed "I'm sorry I hurt your feelings" is way different from actually taking responsibility. Taking responsibility means: *speaking the unarguable truth (S.E.W.) and stepping into a new action.* It might sound like: "I notice that I broke my agreement with you to be here at 6:00 p.m. My stomach feels tight and my jaw is clenched. I feel scared we might have a fight. I'm mad because I wanted to stay at work longer. No, I'm actually mad because I'm working more than I want to. I want to sit down and talk to you about my schedule and my job." Or, for the second example, "I notice my whole body is tense. I feel mad, sad, and scared. I said things that I don't like. I didn't choose to take a time-out, which has really helped me in the past. I recommit to using time-outs when I go into Reactive Brain."

> Anytime we blame, we are giving away our power.

Do you see how taking responsibility actually allows me to check in with my body, find the real issue, and create actual change?

I recommend people stop apologizing and start taking responsibility. And, by the way, I still say "Sorry . . . sorry . . ." when I'm stepping over people to get to my seat in the theater.

Taking responsibility: S.E.W. and stepping into a new action.

Taking full responsibility in any interaction is our quickest route back into empowerment.

THREE TOXIC HABITS TO BREAK

chapter 12

Would you like to take some major steps toward moving beyond blame and into flow? If you were to break the following three insidious habits, it would be like clearing dams out of your own personal energy river. Changing these will truly maximize your ability to reconnect, deepen, and reignite—with your partner and with yourself.

Toxic Habit One

If I hurt you enough (through blame, criticism, or contempt), you'll stop doing what I don't want you to do.

Most of us walk around with the belief that punishment changes behavior. And yet, psychologists have known for decades that punishment is the weakest route to behavior change. What most powerfully transforms our own behavior, as well as those around us (partners, kids, four-leggeds) is *giving positive attention and rewarding what we want to have happen.*

Antidotes for Toxic Habit One

» Focus on what you want to have happen.
» Appreciate yourself and your partner for the positives.
» Place yourself on a blame and complaint diet (see this tool on page 108). This is also a powerful activity to do together.

John Gottman found in relationships that last, partners offered five appreciations for every one criticism. In relationships that thrived, the ratio was 20:1.[18]

Toxic Habit Two

Deciding *this should not be happening!* or its corollary *this should not have happened!*

If you want to make yourself really crazy, decide that what is happening should not be happening. "He said he was going to be here by now, and he's *not*. What's the matter with him?" "I shouldn't be feeling scared. What's the matter with me?" "It wasn't supposed to rain today! What's wrong with those weather forecasters?" (You can see how deciding what is happening shouldn't be happening bridges us right to blaming, to how something or someone is *wrong*.)

This way of thinking leads right into what can really stop flow for couples: talking about how what happened shouldn't have happened. Most "processing" couples focus on this. "If you had just remembered to take the car in for an oil change, we wouldn't be sitting out here in the desert with a blown head gasket." "If you had only remembered to pick up the kids, I wouldn't be so mad at you. But you didn't, so I am. (And now I won't speak to you for three days.)" "If you hadn't pouted, I never would have agreed to that." "If I had slowed down for the yellow light, I wouldn't have gotten that ticket. I can't believe how stupid I am!"

John Gottman found in relationships that last, partners offered five appreciations for every one criticism. In relationships that thrived, the ratio was 20:1.

Antidotes for Toxic Habit Two

> » Get present to what is! Life is happening.
> Right here, right now. Your power is here in the
> moment. The past has happened, and there is
> no way to change it.

> » Sure, you get to figure out better agreements
> (chapter 14), but rehashing what someone *should*
> have done makes no sense. (It goes right back to
> Toxic Habit One, where we think if we make a
> good enough point about how someone wronged
> us, we'll change them. We won't. They'll be shut
> down and defensive, and probably won't even hear
> what we're saying.)

Toxic Habit Three

Believing you (or I) should have or could have done something
better.

People do the best they can. Period. Add up how much sleep
we had last night and our blood sugar level and our upbringing
and our genetic makeup and whether we have enough vitamin
D and whether we meditated or decided to watch the news
and—you get who we are in this moment. It's the best we can
do. So looking back to blame each other or ourselves gets us
way off track into self- or other-hate (which takes us back to
Toxic Habit One and Toxic Habit Two).

I learned this principle when I was watching the snowboard-
ing event in the Winter Olympics of 2006. The favorite for the
gold medal in the women's event (Lindsey Jacobellis) was way
ahead, so far ahead that she did a hotdog move toward the end,
grabbing her board. And falling. I imagine her going over that
move over and over since then—"If I only hadn't done that I
would have gotten the gold!" But she did that. And she didn't
get the gold. And doing that was the sum total of thousands of
hours of practice, the best coaching in the world, a physique

that was attended to by fabulous trainers, and high quality food. It was the best she could do.

And you're doing the best you can. And so is your partner. And so am I.

Antidotes for Toxic Habit Three

» Forgive us all for being human (and for having Reactive Brains).
» Put your attention on "what can I learn from this?"
» Appreciate what is. We all function better when we feel relaxed and in flow. Being loved and appreciated brings out the absolute best in us.

TOOL   COMMITTING TO BLAMING OR TO TAKING RESPONSIBILITY

Decide which commitment you'd like to make:

I commit to blaming others or myself when there is a problem and to putting my energy into figuring out who is good and who is bad.

or

I commit to choosing to be the source in every interaction, taking 100 percent responsibility for creating it.

Now make the commitment by speaking it out loud. Write it down in your journal.
It's a powerful one.

TOOL   MOVING FROM BLAME TO POWER

(Adapted from "The Responsibility Two-Step"[19] by Gay and Kathlyn Hendricks)

Complain and blame about an issue for one to two minutes. Notice what your body feels like. Then shift into these statements (speak the stem out loud and finish it three to four times):

How I keep this issue going is

How I create this is

What I can learn from this is

What I wonder about is

What I really want is

What did you notice about what changed in your body? If you compare how you felt between the complaining and blaming part of the exercise and the taking responsibility part, which internal state feels more familiar? Which did you prefer?

TOOL   BLAME AND COMPLAINT LOG

Keep a "blame and complaint" log for a day. Carry around your journal and write down every time you blame or complain about anything or anyone (including yourself), either verbally or mentally. At the end of the day, go through each blame and complaint and rewrite it, taking full responsibility. (For example, "the weather is crappy, cold and gray and rainy" would become "I felt mad. I wanted the weather to be different from what it was.")

Blame/Complaint	Statement of Responsibility

TOOL   BLAME AND COMPLAINT DIET[20]

Commit to not blaming or complaining for some amount of time (five minutes, a day, a month, forever). See what results you create—do you feel any differently about your partner, yourself, your life? (By the way, a commitment isn't a promise. If you drift back into blaming or complaining, simply recommit to your diet.)

I will not blame or complain for _____ (minutes/hours/days).

Results I Notice:

Would you like to try a move that will exponentially expand your consciousness? Try going on a blame and complaint diet even in your thoughts!

I will not blame or complain in my thoughts or words for _____ (minutes/hours/days).

Results I Notice:

TOOL   HOW DO I KNOW I'M TAKING 100 PERCENT RESPONSIBILITY?

» I'm making *requests.* (not complaining)

» I'm asking *"how am I creating this?"* (not blaming)

» I feel *curious, open, and wondering.* (not focusing on being right)

» I'm giving everyone the *space* for their own experience. (not rescuing)

» I feel a sense of *balance.* (not resentful)

» I'm focused on *appreciation.* (not criticism)

» I'm in the *flow.* (not trying to control)

» I'm making *great agreements* that I'm happy to keep. (not placating and not blaming the agreement breaker)

I feel playful, engaged, open, and alive!

[please copy this and post as a reminder!]

EMPOWERMENT THROUGH INTEGRITY

chapter 13

100% Power = 100% Integrity

Remember a time when you felt powerful. What were you doing? Was it a physical activity, like shooting a hoop, riding a bike, dancing? Was it when you felt successful at something, so you were being acknowledged in some way? Had you just completed something difficult? Or perhaps you were just in the flow of life, watching it all unfold.

The first question here is, what *is* power, really? We certainly have many images of powerful people: the successful business magnate who has many people answering to her; the wealthy person who runs an empire of employees and household help, all of whom do his bidding; the general, president, governor, pope, or other person of influence.

Let's look at this more carefully, though. Do these people actually *feel* powerful? What does it even mean to feel or be powerful?

Try the following ideas out in your body to see if they fit for you. Do any of them match your experience of what feeling powerful *actually* feels like?

» Expressing what you want and being heard

» Getting what you want

» Having a sense of efficacy in the world, taking action, and getting results

» Not being afraid

» Being in alignment with your essence and purpose in the world

» Having an internal sense of being in flow, at peace, and alive

» Feeling connected, known by, and intimate with others

TOOL   WHAT DOES FEELING POWERFUL ACTUALLY FEEL LIKE?

Jot some notes down in your journal about your actual experience of power.

True Power

I'm guessing that after taking your time to reflect on when you've felt powerful, you noticed that your sense of feeling powerful is an internal experience, rather than one to be measured externally through your status. In fact, this view of power is a reflection of what I see as the coming shift in how the interpersonal world operates. Whereas we all are familiar with the hierarchical, patriarchal, "power-over/power-under" model of relationship, the work you're learning here supports the seismic change to a "power-with" way of relating that rests on a foundation of equality. Further, it brings connection into the equation. It assumes that *we are not truly powerful in the world unless we feel intimate with and known by our intimate others.*

I'll explore this paradigm shift more later. Right now let's look more carefully at how to maximize that internal sense of empowerment, even and especially when in relationship. Many of us are pretty darn good at feeling powerful when we're by ourselves; the true challenge occurs when we try to feel just as internally empowered when we're relating to others.

These are the elements that I have discovered lead to that internal sense of empowerment. Some of them must sound familiar to you by now.

> » Expressing what is true for you in the
>   moment and being fully heard and validated
>   for your experience
> » Moving out of the "dense" emotions of mad,
>   sad, and scared into greater expansiveness
> » Being in flow with life, internally and externally
> » Manifesting one's heart desires
> » Having deep connection, passion, and
>   expansiveness in your intimate relationships

Integrity

Maybe you're getting pretty good at feeling your emotions and expressing them. As you may have noticed, however, there's a whole necessary next step, which is deciding what actions to take. To choose actions that are aligned with your essential self, you must be in *integrity*. That is, your feelings, beliefs, words, and actions are all lined up, in resonance with each other and with your deepest self.

Integrity means being fully whole, at one with your true self and committed to living from your essential nature.

Integrity means being fully whole, at one with your true self and committed to living from your essential nature.

This may seem like a tall order, but the work you have been doing up to now in this workbook (speaking unarguably, letting your feelings flow, tuning into what your body is telling you, and translating it into what you really want) is all in preparation for this movement into full integrity. You will know if you're in alignment with yourself when your body feels open and expanded; you'll get unmistakable signals of being out of integrity when your body closes down and contracts. More concretely, you can unearth integrity issues by keeping track of agreements you have made (with yourself and others) that you haven't followed through on, lies you have told, and incompletions in your relationships. Each one of these is a power leak, keeping you from being as big and energized as you might otherwise be.

Here are some examples of people who have found themselves to be out of integrity:

» Bill didn't want to face his money issues, so he stacked up the bills in his drawer, where he wouldn't have to see them or think about them.
» Sue told her community group that she'd help with the fundraiser. When they called her, she just never called them back.

» Janice agreed with her husband that she'd clean her hair out of the sink but was so busy she just "forgot" to.

» Michael decided to not tell his wife about his big attraction to his colleague to "not hurt her feelings."

» Jorge stopped talking to his father two years ago after his dad didn't send him a check he'd promised; he never told his dad why.

» Phyllis promised herself she'd start an exercise program. Tomorrow.

» (Fill in your example of being out of integrity here.) _____

Do you see how energy just leaks away, as the issue takes up our inner space (even if we try never to think about it), and we don't step into our emotional experience and take action?

One reason for our integrity leaks are "shoulds." We can fill our lives with the actions we think we *should* be taking. Whenever we think of a should, however, we are actually trying to apply someone else's ideas to our lives. "Should" is always someone else's idea. Our bodies will tell us what we *want* to do. As long as we're not in Reactive Brain, we can trust that our desires are our own personal built-in compass indicating the path that is truly a reflection of our authenticity.

Thus, indicators of living in integrity are that you

» only make agreements you want to make;

» clear up agreements you've made that you haven't followed through on;

» speak the truth, clear up any lies you have told, and speak your withholds; and

» make sure your actions consist of what you *want* to do, versus what you *should* do.

"Should" is always someone else's idea.

TOOL   DIALING YOURSELF INTO YOUR LIFE

What percentage of your life is devoted to what you *should* be doing? _____ %

What percentage of your life is devoted to what you *want* to be doing? _____ %

What would you like these to be?   Should: _____ %

                                          Want: _____ %

TOOL   INTEGRITY INVENTORY

List all of the parts of your life that you believe are out of integrity: agreements you haven't completed or would like to renegotiate; truths you haven't spoken; shoulds that you might move out of your life. For each item, make an action plan and a commitment for carrying it out. Then revisit this page in your journal, and place a checkmark in the third column for each item that you are now in alignment with.

Item (out of integrity)	Plan	Complete?

Making Great and Successful Agreements

Making great agreements is an art form. Trust is built or broken around agreements that are kept or not kept. Whether or not we keep our agreements is quietly (or sometimes noisily) noted by those around us, who view our character through the lens of Do we do what we say we're going to do? Do we not do what we say we're not going to do?

What I've determined, after decades of working with agreements, is

> a great agreement is one where everyone
> gets everything they want.

Making great agreements where each person gets everything she wants creates the foundation of a relationship. On the other hand, relationships end over poor agreements. As couples weave their relationships over time, from dating to living together long-term, there are thousands of agreements that each person must feel good about. From time agreements to household chores to money to sex to in-laws to child-rearing to free time to friends (and of course, the all-important

> A great
> agreement is one
> where everyone
> gets everything
> they want.

agreements about the toothpaste tube and which way the toilet paper hangs), making great agreements will lead either to fulfillment and flow or resentment, power struggle, and deadlock.

As you've worked through this workbook, you've laid the groundwork for making great and successful agreements. You

> » have committed to being happy instead of being right;
> » know how to discern your body sensations, so you can tune into how you feel and what you want;
> » know when you're in Reactive Brain and how to use shift moves to get back to Creative Brain; and
> » are letting go of blame and stepping into full responsibility.

(Wow, did you know you'd done all that? OK, I didn't say you'd *mastered* it . . . yet.)

Splendid agreements are the result of both (or all) people believing that their desires have been heard and attended to. On the other hand, broken agreements generally occur for a host of reasons. Here are some of those reasons:

> » One or both people were half-hearted while making the agreement.
> » One was placating the other to avoid a fight or to go do something more fun than sitting around processing.
> » There are hidden resentments.
> » There are power dynamics coming forward (i.e., the one experiencing low-power isn't saying what he wants, or the person in the high-power position is demanding she gets what she wants).
> » Wheedling, cajoling, criticizing, browbeating, eye-rolling got the other person to give up what he really wanted.

Do you want an amazing relationship that neither one of you would ever want to leave? Here's how to do that: make sure you both get want you want. Do you want a relationship where one or both of you gets sick of the whole thing? Here's how you do that: rely on short-term strategies to keep the peace without taking the time to sort through how to ensure each person gets what he or she wants.

Have I convinced you to try a new way of making agreements? Then, here we go.

The process of coming to a successful agreement can be one of the most co-creative of a relationship, as the big, interesting question is,

How can we both get everything we want?

Does that sound wacky? I expect it does based on the pretty consistent reactions I have gotten in the past when I proposed this idea. People are just not used to a co-creative mode of relating, where we get to be equal partners in creating new ideas and solutions. Welcome to this new world!

Let me walk you through some important ideas about making really great agreements, the kind that will support both of you to express your full selves and thrive together.

Delete the Word *Compromise* from Your Brain

OK, I know it isn't quite that easy. But this persistent relationship ideal of compromise gives people the message that they should give up half of what they want and be happy about it. That's a short-term strategy that leads to long-term resentment and a life that is half lived. As you learn the process below, you'll see that if you put the tools you're learning to use, it really is possible for everyone to get everything they want. And that leads to terrific, fulfilling relationships.

Take a moment and really try out the following idea in your body. It might sound strange, especially if you've ever had the experience of having to fight for what you want. Here it is:

So long as you got *everything* you want, would it be OK
with you if your partner got everything she or he wants?

Read that through again. Talk to your body about it. Feel the
relaxation that can come with the idea of you getting everything you want. Breathe into the spaciousness of realizing you
don't have to compete or compromise or give up or give in.
Instead, your task is to stay in the expansiveness of Creative
Brain until you find the new idea, the one that you each like so
well that it's easy to agree to and implement.

Making Agreements Is a Team Sport

Each person is 100 percent responsible for making a great
agreement. That means that strategies people have tradition-
ally relied on to get our way (whining, cajoling, demanding,
wheedling, pressuring, withdrawing, stonewalling, "forgetting,"
going dumb, resisting, manipulating, bargaining, arguing,
giving up) aren't actually useful here. In this new world of great
and successful agreements, finding what works for both people
is the team goal. That requires each person to show up, be clear,
be unarguable, and follow through with what she or he agrees
to. It also means this radical notion:

If an agreement is broken,
both people are responsible for the broken agreement.

OK, I know I just lost some of you here. Remember that my
goal is that you both feel empowered, alive, and in integrity.
Knowing that you each are responsible for any agreement that
doesn't work gives you your power back. (Notice the alternative:
browbeating your partner until he or she is "more responsible."
Not exactly a pathway toward fun and connection, is it?)

So if you're the one who might have kept score over time
(you know, the righteous "I always keep my agreements. I just

So long as
you got *everything*
you want,
would it be
OK with you
if your
partner got
everything she
or he wants?

do not understand how my partner can be so irresponsible and childish to break his!"), it's time to step back and stop blaming. Your power lies in understanding what *you're* doing to create unsuccessful agreements. And to start doing something that actually gets your team to the goal.

And what if you're the irresponsible, childish agreement-breaker? Time to get vertical. Come to the table. Say what you want and what you don't want, and stick with it until you and your partner find a solution that truly nourishes both of you, even if that means standing in the heat of your partner's reaction when you speak your truth.

Signs That You're the Righteous Scorekeeper

You notice that you

> » nag,
> » police,
> » remind,
> » criticize,
> » track your partner's moves, or
> » sound or feel parental.

Signs That You're the Irresponsible Agreement-Breaker

You notice that you

> » avoid,
> » placate,
> » justify,
> » whine,
> » cover your tracks, or
> » sound or feel childlike.

> If an agreement is broken, both people are responsible for the broken agreement.

Great Agreements Are the Basis for Creating Trust

We watch each other. We notice whether the other person is doing what she says she's going to do, or not doing what he

This *is not* about justifying a want. ("Because I want it" is really the best reason there is.)

says he's not going to do. We notice that about ourselves. So agreements matter. They form your internal integrity and the integrity of your relationships. So pay attention:

>> Do what you say you're going to do.
>> Don't do what you say you're not going to do.
>> Take care to renegotiate agreements that aren't working for you.[21]

Halt! Stop Any Agreement-Making Process When Someone Goes into Reactive Brain

Reactive Brain will only generate old and rigid ideas, not new solutions. Finding the brand-new idea, the one that could potentially meet everyone's wants, requires Creative Brain. If and when one or the other of you notices you're in Reactive Brain, the very best use of your time is to *stop trying to solve the problem.* It is unsolvable from Reactive Brain, otherwise you would have solved it. Instead, use your time and energy wisely by doing everything you can to shift into Creative Brain. (This would be a good time to get out your journal or go back to chapter 9 to review your favorite shift moves.)

So let's get to the nuts and bolts of making a great and successful agreement.

First, notice the signs that an agreement is necessary. These might include resentment, frustration, confusion about expectations, and an overall sense of spinning your wheels.

Then, when preparing to make an agreement, take a moment to ground yourself. Breathe. Be in your body. Move around, flap your arms, wiggle your hips. Ground yourself in Creative Brain, generating a sense of expansiveness and possibility in your body. Remind yourself that the goal is not for one person to win and the other to lose, but to co-create a wonderful new way of being that reflects both of you and the best of your relationship.

The first step in making a good agreement is *for both people to state the bottom-line quality of exactly what they want,*

> » not what each thinks the other wants or does
>   not want,
> » not what each thinks the "right way" is or should
>   be, and
> » not what someone else wants,

but the *bottom-line quality.*

Getting to the bottom line is the key step. It can take some time to get to what this is. For example, "I want to paint the house green" might shift to "I want to look at our house and feel soothing inside." "I want you to help around the house" might become "I want to be your equal and teammate in our relationship." "I don't want to do any stupid chores during my free time" could be "I want to feel free to make my own choices about how I spend my time."

The next step is for each person to speak the *unarguable truth* about the issue.

This *is not* about justifying a want.
("Because I want it" is really the best reason there is.)

It *is* about trying to be clear about what is going on,
so the other person can understand.

It *is* about trying to be clear about what is going on, so the other person can understand.

The unarguable truth (sensations, emotions, wants) around agreements sounds like: "When I look around the house, my body feels tight. I feel scared that I'm alone in making sure it is orderly. Oh, even more, I'm afraid of other people's judgments when they come inside. What I really want is to be your equal and to know that we're on the same team. And I want to feel peaceful and calm." The other person's view might be: "As we're talking about this, my stomach feels tight and my jaw is clenched. I feel scared about having a fight with you about this. And I'm afraid of giving up what I really want. And I feel angry about how I've been doing that in my life in general. What I want is to decide how I want to spend my time. And I want to feel connected with you."

Do you see how dropping into the unarguable truth starts moving you both onto the same team?

Once it is clear to both what each wants, the fun part is brainstorming a list of creative solutions, which is the next step. When you come up with a solution that is big enough for both of you to get most of what you want, you'll know it, because

> » you'll be able to breathe,
> » it will feel like the solution is part of the flow, and
> » your body will be relaxed and open.

When you come up with a possible agreement, check: *Can you both hold yourselves fully accountable to following through with it?* If so, agree to it. Appreciate yourselves for your creativity. Throw in a high-five!

Here's an example of this process at work (though it's almost never this linear):

Peyton: "When I look around the house, my body feels tight. I feel scared that I'm alone in making sure it is orderly. Oh, even more, I'm afraid of other people's judgments if they came inside. What I really want is to be your equal and to know that we're on the same team. And I want to feel peaceful and calm."

Chris: "As we're talking about this, my stomach feels tight and my jaw is clenched. I feel scared about having a fight with you about this. And I'm afraid of giving up what I really want. And I feel angry about how I've been doing that in my life in general. What I

want is to decide how I want to spend my time.
And I want to feel connected with you."

Peyton: "I want that, too."

Chris: "Yeah, I want to be equals and teammates, too.
And I like the peaceful and calm thing."

(Note that when you get to the bottom line, both people almost always want the same thing.)

Peyton: "So, how can we both get what we want?"

Chris: "Now that we've talked about it, I feel a lot better. I think that I was just avoiding thinking about housework so I wouldn't have to deal with it. And, now that I think about it, I want to have more fun with you. I have the story that our lives are full of 'shoulds' and not so much about being creative."

Peyton: "Yeah, I notice that I'm more relaxed just talking about it. Maybe what I really wanted was just to connect with you, to know we're in this together."

Chris: "OK, so what I really want is to have more fun and see what happens with the housework."

Peyton: "I appreciate how you bring up the fun thing. I want to have fun with you. And I plan to just do what I want and stop policing what you do. And I want to be more creative in my life in general."

Chris: "OK, good. How about our agreement is that we plan some fun this week, and see what happens with the housework?"

Peyton: "Yes! Let's play around with creating that backyard art we've been talking about."

Chris: "Yes! I'm there."

What I find is that this process is necessary to just determine what the real problem is. For Peyton and Chris, it actually had nothing to do with the housework; it was an issue of fun and creativity. When I work with couples, I avoid even talking about solutions until they've used the unarguable truth to get to what is the real issue to be solved.

What about Really Big Agreements?

Having a baby. Moving for one person's job . . . again. Having family move in. Selling everything to live on a sailboat. How does this process work for the really big decisions?

The process itself is the same. Each person takes time and space to get down to the bottom-line truth about how she feels and what she really wants. The difference for really big decisions is that it might take longer to get there: more wandering into old patterns that are apt to be clouding up the conversation; more time to feel to the very core; and more space to remember that you are allies on the same team. Give yourselves space to seesaw back and forth, letting each person try on the other side of the coin. Build in a whole lot of breathing, moving, and wondering, until your body tells you the whole truth and you're able to openheartedly hear your partner's.

TOOL   GETTING TO THE BOTTOM LINE

Practice going from what you think you want to the bottom-line quality of what you want. Start small; as you get better at this, you can go bigger and bigger and find out what you really want.

Examples:

I Think I Want	Bottom-Line Quality
A sandwich for lunch.	Something I feel satisfied by; something that I can chew.
A vacation to Hawaii.	To feel warm and spacious, expanded and relaxed.
An open relationship.	Do what I want to do when I want to do it.

Now you try it. Get out your journal and make two columns and fill them in.

I Think I Want	Bottom-Line Quality

To end where we began: great agreements are an art form, one that you might never even have seen before. Give yourself and your relationship team time and space—to become impeccable with your agreements, to use this process, to fail, and then try again. These skills build over time. Eventually, you'll find the confidence that comes from knowing that you can trust yourself and each other. That will be wonderful, solid ground that you can stand on. Together.

TOOL   MAKING A GREAT AND SUCCESSFUL AGREEMENT

This tool contains everything I've been walking you through, so give yourselves plenty of practice with it. Take it slowly. And when you can get all the way through the steps, please celebrate—you've just crossed the bridge to a radically alive relationship!

1. Take a moment to breathe and remind yourselves that the goal is to come up with a really creative solution that reflects the best of both of you and in which you can both get everything you want.

2. Person 1 states the bottom-line *quality* of what he wants and the unarguable truth about the issue. Then Person 2 does the same thing. Make a list of all of these qualities.

Stop the process if either of you go into Reactive Brain.
Use shift moves to get back to Creative Brain. Do this as often as is necessary.

Take your time in getting to the bottom line. It will be worth it.

3. Brainstorm a list of creative solutions that incorporate the qualities of what you each want. Push yourselves to come up with some that might seem crazy or off-the-wall so you can really stretch out into the wide expanse of Creative Brain. Have some fun with this.

4. Decide which solution is big enough for both of you to get what you want. Can you both breathe? Do your bodies feel expansive? Does this agreement seem to be easy to carry out?

5. Check this solution: Can you both hold yourselves fully accountable to following through with it? If so, bravo! You've made a great agreement.

6. Writing your agreement down can be very helpful, especially for the stickier issues. (You may want to have a Relationship Agreement Journal to track what you've come up with.)

Once you've tried out the agreement, it may need to be modified. Like an engine that is designed in the lab but then needs to be taken on a test drive, adjustments and tweaks are inevitable. It is the responsibility of each person to ask the other to renegotiate the agreement if it needs to be adjusted (which could be ongoing, as even the most carefully constructed agreements can run aground when put into practice). To keep the power of agreements alive in a relationship, both people must agree to any change (versus what people are tempted to do, which is to simply say to themselves, "I never liked that agreement anyway, so I'm just not going to follow it").

FROM POWER STRUGGLE TO EMPOWERMENT

chapter 15

What would happen if we were as big as we are?

What would happen if we were as big as we are?

By this point in this workbook, you probably have a sense of where we're headed. I believe that people thrive in relationships in which they can express their deepest, most essential selves in an ongoing way. In this context, honesty is the highest priority, as living from essence requires a continuous expression of oneself as experienced through one's body sensations. Like a very sensitive steering mechanism, the body gives us ongoing authenticity feedback through its sensations, which can be translated into emotions and desires. Conscious relationship requires tuning into these sensations, translating them, speaking them in a way that the other person can hear, and choosing one's actions accordingly.

The old relationship paradigm of hierarchy, that is, "power-over/power-under," doesn't give much room for any of these possibilities. Instead, the old structure thrives on one person taking control while the other gives it up. The "compromise" that we're taught to expect in relationship leads to keeping an ongoing scorecard: I gave up what I wanted the last time, so this time it's your turn to give up what you want. Or maybe we'll each decide to let go of half of what we really want. No wonder long-term relationship has such a reputation for people settling into the long sleep of unconsciousness, as people must disconnect from themselves (and therefore from each other) to live in this half life.

Another big problem with hierarchy and power-over is that no one really feels that powerful. Anyone who is in a one-up position, the one who apparently feels the most powerful, can attest to this. Maintaining power over someone else requires constant effort at monitoring compliance and having to support the one in the "weaker" position. In this traditional model (which is really based on a parent-child dynamic), a boss has to watch employees carefully to make sure they are doing their jobs, the sergeant has to yell at the privates, and the coach has to be all over the players. The boss, sergeant, and coach don't get to relax and be in flow, as one of their underlings is apt to mess up at any point. Power struggle is built in to this whole setup, as the forced influence of the one "in charge" is bound to get predictable responses from those being ordered around: passive-aggressive behaviors, childlike compliance, or out-and-out rebellion. (To get a sense of this, talk to the parent of an adolescent to see how powerful he or she feels.)

"Power-over" gets to be in charge but has to use up lots of energy monitoring and pushing the sometime obedient, often resistant "power-under." Meanwhile, the power-under can just follow along and be taken care of by the dominant one, but at the cost of his or her sense of power and efficacy. While we're used to this chain-of-command in the military, it creates terrible problems in intimacy, where people generally want to be seen for who they really are, to feel deep emotional connection, and to be met by someone they respect as an equal.

The alternative to this whole outdated paradigm is that of being nonhierarchical and power-with in relationship. There is no "better-than" or "worse-than"; everyone is considered equally valuable at his or her essence. Power struggle becomes unnecessary, as the interesting, creative question becomes "how can we both get everything we want?" (Sound familiar?) It is no longer a competition, with the winner taking all and the loser licking his wounds, but an ongoing sense of co-creation, as the goal is for all to express their best, most essential selves.

Whereas this new model of relationship makes intuitive sense, it is still unusual in the world of intimacy. What most of us still embody is what is most familiar to us from growing up: the parent-child way of relating. We've watched how our parents took charge and directed, ruling the roost by doling out rewards and punishments. We carry the experience of having been dependent children, so know what power-under feels like in its compliance, giving up self, and being rebellious. Stepping into equality, where both (or all) people have the room to express their needs and wants and then have the support to effectively meet these needs, could be something we've never actually seen or experienced.

To give you a better idea of what this new paradigm actually looks like, imagine this: Your daily life is one where you and your partner relate from your essential selves. You walk through the world in connection with your own authenticity, expressing who you truly are in the creative endeavors of work, play, and relationship. When you experience triggered emotions, you each can describe what is going on, and move through your feelings without blaming anybody else. Your inner world is filled with aliveness, and you are connected to flow. You create deep connection and intimacy by being able to speak the bottom-line truth at any given time in a way that the other person can hear nondefensively. As you each develop your own inner power, one person's bigness does not threaten the other. In this world of equality, the thrill comes from each of you embodying your divine nature and observing as the whole world benefits from the expression of your full selves.

How does that sound to you? Promising? Maybe even something to strive for?

So take your image one step further: the vision of equality is for each of you to be fully in your own power. That is, each of you is 100 percent powerful. Another way to express this is to say that each is 100 percent responsible for your own life, and so for what is occurring in the relationship.

It can be pretty easy to get out of this balance though, can't it? When one person takes on more than 100 percent responsibility and the other less, you are right back in the world of power-over/power-under.

Taking Less Than 100 Percent Power or Responsibility

> Anytime we take less than 100 percent power or responsibility, we're in the *victim* position.

Yes, *anytime*. That means, whenever we blame *anything* (our partner; our boss; the weather; the traffic; even our bad, loser selves) for what's going on in our lives, we've taken on the victim role. We're stepping into power-under.

Let's get concrete here. What does this look like and sound like? Here are some examples:

"Why can't I ever get a break?"

"Why do these things always happen to me?"

"There's nothing I can do about this."

"Why do you have to be so mean?"

"If you loved me, you wouldn't treat me this way."

Anytime we take less than 100 percent power or responsibility, we're in the *victim* position.

"You've really hurt me."

"(People/the world/the other political party or gender/ some other group) (suck/don't care/are jerks/are ruining everything)."

Fill in your own; let yourself be really whiny about it:

Notice how these statements are actually just complaints. Also tune into their childlike tone. They carry the sense of the speaker being one down to some authority outside of him.

So by saying these are victim statements, do I mean that no one is ever victimized? Of course not. Children are by definition dependent so are quite vulnerable to victimization. Bad things—rape, muggings, robberies, fires—happen to adults. But allowing ourselves to stay in the victim position over time is a toxic invitation to the worst internal misery we know. Being willing to ask, *under any circumstance,* the key question of "how did I create this?" bridges us back into the world of feeling powerful and in charge of our lives.

Taking More Than 100 Percent Power or Responsibility

For every person who takes less than his 100 percent, there is another who takes more. The more than 100 percent responsibility (a.k.a., power-over) position looks and sounds parental, as we culturally legitimize parents to control situations. There are two broad categories of taking control: through *nurturance* and through *aggression.* Here's what each sounds like.

TOOL   HOW I CREATED THIS/WHAT I'LL DO DIFFERENTLY

Get out your journal. Remember a recent event that you felt upset about and write it at the top of the page. Now make a list of "I created this by . . . " For example, yesterday I had a conflict with my partner while we were walking our dogs. Here's what my list of "How did I create this?" reads: I created this by

1. reacting to her words;
2. taking what she said personally;
3. having old feelings in my body that were unprocessed;
4. not breathing;
5. not choosing to use shift moves; and
6. seeing her as my enemy and forgetting that she was my ally.

I'll stop there, but note that the more I can unearth about how I created an issue, the more places I have to do something different. (In fact, I tell my clients that these lists are like gold, as they are direct lines to where you have real power, that is, in how you can change right this minute. They could save you years of therapy.) In my list above, I can focus on

1. letting myself look at how I react;
2. remembering that her reaction has nothing to do with me;
3. processing the old feelings that come up around this pattern;
4. remembering to breathe—deeply;
5. recommitting to using shift moves; and
6. remembering my partner is my ally, that we're on the same team.

OK, your turn. Here are the headings for your lists:

Issue	How I Created This Issue	What I Can Do Differently

Controlling through Nurturing

"How can I help you?"

"What do you need?"

"Are you hungry? Do you want something to eat?"

"Good job! What a good boy you are!"

Controlling through Aggression

"That's the wrong way to do that."

"Quit it. You're being (insensitive/ridiculous/foolish/etc.)."

"Why didn't you eat before we left? I told you you'd
be hungry."

"I can't believe you lost your wallet again. When are
you going to get it together?"

"I think this is about your issues with your mother."

Notice how easy it is for control through nurturance to start sliding into control through aggression. That progression sounds something like this:

"Do you want to eat before we go? No? Are you sure?
You might want to remember the last time, when you
got hungry. You got kind of whiny. In fact, you made
lots of people uncomfortable; you were so unpleasant.
I *wish* you would *eat!* What's the matter with you,
why can't you plan ahead?"

Now it's easy to see how people taking less than 100 percent responsibility and those taking more can easily lock together. One leads to the next to the next:

"I'm hungry."

"You want me to make you something?"

"Naw, I'll be OK."

"No, really, I'll make it for you."

"No, I don't want to eat what you make."

"It's good for you! And you know what happens when you don't eat."

"I said I'm not hungry!"

"You don't have to be so snappy about it. Geez."

Are you willing to fully hear the other person's response without doing anything to change his or her experience?

Once we get out of balance with less than and more than 100 percent responsibility, these dynamics seem to take on a life of their own, like an itsy-bitsy-spider chain of who is taking on the parent role and who is being childlike. Reactive Brain, and our pack-animal instinct to resort to hierarchy under threat, is the culprit for getting this chain started at all. And once we're in those reactions, it can be really tough to shift out of them.

Generally each partner shifts back and forth between taking on less and more than his or her 100 percent, mostly because he or she doesn't know about the pitfalls of being out of whack. Most of us expect that this power-over/power-under seesaw is what relationship just looks and feels like. And this is a main source of the dimming of life energy, self-expression, and sexuality that can impact long-term relationships, as it's pretty tough to have passionate connection when you're feeling like a parent or a child.

Am I saying you should never be nurturing? Of course not. The ongoing checking in on each other, "How are you doing?" "How does this feel to you?" is what provides the oil to the engine of relationship. But notice how it's a slippery slope from checking in to controlling. The tipping point can be found with this question:

> Are you willing to fully hear the other person's response without doing anything to change his or her experience?

It is the job of the parent to mold the child into a good, productive citizen by monitoring and correcting her behavior. While this is clearly no longer appropriate in a relationship between adults, few of us have observed anything different from this. As Gay and Katie Hendricks observe, any relationship that is not of equals is simply an entanglement.[22] Shifting out of entanglement into equality and full-adult status requires embodying the beliefs that no one else gets to (or needs to) control us or judge us, that we don't get to control anyone else, and that it is up to each of us to be our own internal authority.

> People in relationships must be able to influence each other. There is a big difference between influence (which happens when we speak from our emotional being) and control (when we get parental).

People in relationships must be able to influence each other. There is a big difference between influence (which happens when we speak from our emotional being) and control (when we get parental).

TOOL   HOW I TRY TO CONTROL OTHERS

Here's a secret: we're all controlling. We may try to control directly, by using declarative language ("Be sure you remember your lunch." "Stop doing that"). Or we might be indirect or manipulative by implying the other is wrong ("People who do [x] are weak/irresponsible/need to get a life." "I can't believe you did [y]"). We can even control through our own collapse ("I know! I'm awful. Just shoot me.") Letting yourself know your own favorite strategies for trying to control others can be freeing.

Watch yourself in the next day. Journal about your favorite ways to try to control other people.

JUDGMENT AND DEFENSE

chapter 16

Some people seem to believe that one of their duties in a relationship is to judge the other. The gist of conversations sound like this: "Are you wearing *that*?" "Wow, you've really put on some pounds." "You're a slob." "I can't believe what an insensitive lout you are."

And what is the natural response to others' judgment? We defend ourselves.

Clearly, I've been unsuccessful at publicizing what I believe are the privileges endowed to each one of us when we reach adulthood:

When you're an adult, no one gets to judge you.

**And when you're an adult,
you don't have to defend yourself.**

So no one gets to judge you, not even your mother, and for sure, not your partner.

It's one of those hard habits to break. We get so confused by how to be a good partner. We start to think we're supposed to control the other person, improve them. We forget that we fell in love with them as they were and that they chose us for all of ourselves.

When you're an adult, no one gets to judge you.

> **And when you're an adult, you don't have to defend yourself.**

(The comedienne Suzanne Westenhoefer says: "We meet some-one, we fall in love with who they are, we start to notice their issues and pressure them to change. Then we tell them, 'I have to leave you—you're no longer the person I fell in love with!'")

Well, what about how our partner's choices affect us? That drinking problem that's getting worse, the workaholism, the cigarettes, or other drifts—shouldn't we say something?

Sure. How about something—unarguable? And how about replacing defensiveness with the same skill, adding some open-ness and authenticity?

Let's take another drive down S.E.W. lane, get some more prac-tice. Can you make these judgments unarguable? I'll get you started.

TOOL   PRACTICING MOVING OUT OF JUDGMENT

Arguable (remember, you can tell something is arguable because someone can argue with you): "Are you wearing that?"

Unarguable: "I notice my stomach is in a knot. I'm afraid that someone at the party will judge me. I have a story that you should wear something besides sweat pants. And, really, I know that you're 100 percent responsible for what you decide to wear."

Arguable: "You've really put on some pounds."

Unarguable:

Arguable: "You're a slob."

Unarguable:

Arguable: "You're an insensitive lout."

Unarguable:

Now let's try the other side of this, practicing nondefensive responses.

Possible response to "Are you wearing that?"

"Wow. My face feels flushed. I feel angry and scared. [Breathing and moving for a couple of minutes.] OK, that's moving through. I want to wear what I want to wear. I wonder what you're feeling?"

Ready to try the others?

TOOL   PRACTICING MOVING OUT OF DEFENSIVENESS

"You've really put on some pounds."

Nondefensive Response:

"You're a slob."

Nondefensive Response:

Arguable: "You're an insensitive lout."

Nondefensive Response:

Let's take it up a notch, to the really tough stuff to talk about. How about a conversation about a drift? Let's go for broke, talk about a partner's possible addiction.

Here's the old way:

> "Honey, it's time I tell you—you have a drinking problem."

> "It's none of your business. I'm out of here."

Now let's try it from both directions. Let's start with the concerned partner:

> "I'd like to talk to you about something that's really important to me. I notice my whole body feels shaky. I feel afraid to talk about this. I'm feeling less connected with you. I'm not sure what that's about. I want to feel connected. My story is that I lose connection with you when you've been using alcohol, but I'm not sure. I'm wondering about it all. What do you think?"

And from the other person's perspective:

> "OK, give me a couple of minutes. I just got really tensed up. [Walking around.] Now I'm ready to listen. I feel afraid, though. I'm afraid you're judging me, telling me what to do. Hmmm, no, really I'm afraid that I'm going to have to give up some control. Aw, hell, I'm just afraid. And I notice I want to be mad. But I feel it in my stomach. [Breathing, moving more.] Alcohol? Yes, let's talk about it. Is there feedback you want to give me?"

These are big conversations. Give yourselves plenty of time to have them. Don't rush through it all; the bridge between

Marital researcher John Gottman has singled out these negative communication patterns as being particularly harmful to relationships: criticism, defensiveness, contempt, and stonewalling.

mind and body needs time to traverse. It can be complicated to translate the language of the body to ourselves, let alone someone else.

Switching from judgment to what is unarguable, from defending ourselves to being authentic, are truly spiritual practices. And leave it to intimate relationships to give us plenty of practice!

Four Horsemen of the Apocalypse
Marital researcher John Gottman has singled out these negative communication patterns as being particularly harmful to relationships: criticism, defensiveness, contempt, and stonewalling.[23]

TOOL   POWER INVENTORY

Do an inventory of your life in terms of where you are power-over, where you are power-under, and where you are power-with.

Signs of Power-Over: You will feel parental. You'll notice your language is nurturing or aggressive (critical, directive), and you'll view the other as childlike, often feeling disrespectful or even contemptuous toward them. When this is way out of balance, you'll probably notice a sense of over-responsibility, seriousness, burden, or resentment.

Signs of Power-Under: You'll feel childlike. Your language might be defensive, one-down, or placating. You might feel secretive, resistive, or rebellious. You'll view the other as controlling and critical. Over time, you'll begin to lose your sense of self and wonder if you really have the skills to make it in the world alone.

Signs of Power-With: You'll feel an internal sense of power: in flow, open, moving toward your goals. Your language is open and respectful. You can state your perspective and what your needs are, and be open to those of the other. You view the other as your equal and know that you are both

(continued on next page)

worthy of deep respect. Discussions lead to increased creativity for both of you, as new ideas and solutions are easily generated.

For the table below, think about the power dynamic in different aspects of your relationship, like how you make decisions about money, children, how time is spent, household chores, etc. Check the column that is closest to your experience: Are you mostly power-under, power-over, or power-with in terms of this issue?

Category	Power-Under	Power-Over	Power-With
Money	❏	❏	❏
Family	❏	❏	❏
Sex	❏	❏	❏
Time	❏	❏	❏
Household management	❏	❏	❏
Children	❏	❏	❏
Friends	❏	❏	❏
Work	❏	❏	❏
Driving	❏	❏	❏
Weather	❏	❏	❏
Your internal state	❏	❏	❏
Food	❏	❏	❏
Other substances	❏	❏	❏
Politics	❏	❏	❏

THE TRIANGLE: GETTING STUCK IN POWER STRUGGLE

chapter 17

When two adults are caught in any parent-child or power-over/ power-under dynamic, *power struggle is inevitable.*

This, really, is the good news. It might seem possible that one person in a relationship has all the control while the other just gives it up to be taken care of. However, if you look below the surface, you'll find the power struggle. *We simply will not allow ourselves to be controlled over time.* We'll comply when we think we have to, then find ways to passively take back control: withdraw, get spacey and "forget" or just "happen" to be late, shut down sexually, shut down emotionally. The "parent," who first might have felt powerful and in control, will inevitably feel frustrated, alone, and despondent. And *not* powerful. The "child" will have moments of triumph when control has been thwarted through a broken agreement, withdrawal, or shutdown, but this is at the cost of her sense of self and her integrity.

Additionally, this parent-child paradigm is the death knell for passionate, co-creative relationship. No adult can afford to give up self, so no one can actually inhabit the child position for very long. Similarly, it is impossible to stay in the parent

We will not allow ourselves to be controlled over time.

position without losing all respect for the childlike adult. As one person overfunctions in a parental way, the other underfunctions, which causes the first to overfunction more. Over time, this becomes more and more polarized, with each person feeling out of balance and increasingly desperate ("whatever happened to the person I fell in love with?"). Neither feels powerful, that's for sure, as neither is getting the relationship that she really wants.

A great illustration of this struggle, and the ensuing entrenched energy of mucky stuckness, is a model that I've found to be extremely useful. It is called the Karpman Drama Triangle and was created back in 1968 by Stephen Karpman.[24] This is what it looks like (Karpman's original titles were *victim, rescuer,* and *persecutor;* Gay and Kathlyn Hendricks updated these to *victim, hero,* and *villain*):

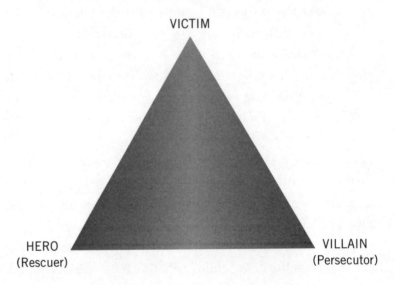

VICTIM

HERO
(Rescuer)

VILLAIN
(Persecutor)

Here are some things to know about the Triangle:

» It is the anatomy of any power struggle.
» You can enter it from any position (which makes even the hero position, seemingly positive, as problematic as victim and villain).

» Once you're in the Triangle, it can be extremely difficult to move out of it. The contagion of Reactive Brain gives the Triangle its own energy vortex, pulling people in and under—and far away from Creative Brain.

» Each position represents a movement away from 100 percent responsibility. The victim takes less than 100 percent ("I can't do it!"); the hero more than 100 percent ("I'll take care of it/you"); and the villain vacillates between both ("If you weren't so screwed up, I wouldn't have to be criticizing you all the time").

» Once in the Triangle, most people move around position to position (which typically is how big blowups unfold). Most power struggles become a race for the victim position[25] (trying to prove how you hurt me more than I hurt you, so you really are the bad guy).

» You can play out the whole Triangle in your inner world, include one other person, or get many people involved.

» Notice that the whole point of the Triangle is to decide *who is to blame.* Like in any good drama, the hero swoops in to take care of the poor victim who is being attacked by the evil villain. But, since few of us view ourselves as the villain, we have to keep defending ourselves by proving the villain is someone else.

The Karpman Drama Triangle is the perfect illustration of the constriction and entrenchment of the power-over/power-under dynamic. Moving out of it is exactly what is necessary to move back into the expansive, creativity-enhancing land of power-with.

TOOL   BECOMING AWARE OF THE TRIANGLE

Carry your journal with you for a week. Note the positions you typically take. Are you most likely to be in the victim, the hero, or the villain position? How does that change with different people and in different situations?

What I Notice about Me and the Triangle:

TOOL   THE WORLD AND THE TRIANGLE

Observe the world around you: newspaper articles, work situations, family relationships, and interactions you witness. Notice the positions of the Triangle that each person takes.

What I Notice about the World and the Triangle:

Getting Out of the Triangle

Below is the process that allows for movement out of the Triangle (also known as the movement from crappyland to happyland). You'll recognize many of the steps, such as: speaking the unarguable truth, being curious (instead of right), breathing, moving, appreciating, taking full responsibility as the source of what is occurring, and getting to the bottom-line issue.

To get out of the triangle

1. Notice you're in it. (Signs you're in it: You don't feel good. You're in Reactive Brain. You feel stuck.)

2. Decide if you're ready to shift. (This step is really important. Don't push it. If you're not ready or willing to shift, that's a good thing for you and the people around you to know. Just be clear about it. You can hang out in your unwillingness for as long as you want. When you are ready to shift, continue through the rest of the steps.)

3. Give yourself time to complain with your whole body for one to two minutes. (If your complaint concerns your partner, work up to doing this with him or her. Otherwise, you can do this by yourself.) Label your position. Are you the *victim* (with smokescreen feelings of shame, humiliation, embarrassment, pain, confusion, hurt); *villain* (feeling indignation, blame, righteousness); or *hero* (feeling pity, sympathy, apologetic, helpful)?[26]

4. Now step in and use some power moves:
   » Breathe, move, be in your body.
   » Use the Moving Emotions Process
     (you can find it in chapter six).

TOOL   GETTING OUT OF THE TRIANGLE

You can use this process by yourself, you can do it with your partner,* or you can use it to coach someone else. This is another of the really transformative exercises that are in this workbook. Give yourself time to try it out. If you're doing this with a partner, be sure to take it slowly, and remember—*stop and shift if one of you goes into Reactive Brain.*

Create "Victim," "Hero," and "Villain" signs on 8 1/2" x 11" sheets of paper. Lay them out on the floor. Decide on an issue that you want to transform.

1. Ask: "Are you willing to shift?" If not, be clear with yourself and your partner. Come back to do the rest of this process when you are ready.

2. Role-play the typical way this issue plays out, moving around between the Victim, Villain, and Hero cards. Let yourself exaggerate the conflict with your whole body so you can really take on the roles (and actually have some fun with this).

3. Use the shift moves you've learned to shift out of the triangle:

   » Breathe, move, be fully in your body.

   » Use the Moving Emotions Process:
      a. *Notice* the sensation.
      b. *Focus* the sensation.
      c. *Accept* the sensation.
      d. *Expand* the sensation.
      e. *Label* the emotions (mad/sad/scared/glad/sexual).
      f. *Ask.* (What are the sensations/emotions trying to communicate?)
      d. *Move* it (through breathing and moving).
      e. *Celebrate* it.

   » Say something unarguable (sensations, emotions, want).

» Be curious, wonder:

What's the real issue?

What does this remind you of?

What are you doing to create this?

How are you keeping this going?

4. Answer the question: What do you *really* want?

5. Choose an action or make an agreement that has body resonance and is easy to commit to.

When you first try this with your partner, it helps to not currently be in the middle of the conflict.

» Speak an unarguable truth (S.E.W.): a sensation, an emotion, what you want.

» Be curious; wonder what the real issue is.

» Ask: How am I creating this? How am I keeping this going? What does this remind me of?

» Keep breathing and moving until your body tells you what the real, bottom-line issue is.

5. Then, answer this question: What do I really want?

6. Finally, if you're doing this process by yourself, decide on an action step that will take you toward what you really want. If you're doing it with your partner (or others), wait until he's gone through the same process and then come up with an agreement that—you guessed it—allows everyone to get everything they want.

TOOL   KNOWING WHEN YOU'RE IN THE TRIANGLE

List the main signs that you're in Triangle (a.k.a., crappyland and Reactive Brain):

The Triangle is a tool I literally use nearly every day, in my practice and in my personal life. Let yourself fully go into it so you can take the steps to move out of it. If you don't take it too seriously ("Oh no! We're in the Triangle!"), you can even have some fun with it. Melodramas (remember Dudley Do-Right, Snidely Whiplash, and Little Nell?) have been around for a long time, perhaps as long as humans have been able to speak. We wouldn't have action movies if we didn't have victims, villains, and heroes. Letting yourself move around these positions and fully embody them will take you to the real issues that lurk underneath the dramas you might have been playing out all of your life.

TOOL YOUR RELATIONSHIP WELL-BEING BANK ACCOUNT

We are constantly making deposits and withdrawals from our relationship bank account of well-being. Relationships that have positive balances thrive; those that have ongoing debits lead to emotional bankruptcy and, ultimately, the closing of the heart account. When people end relationships, they often say things like "I just don't have the energy anymore," or "I'm out of gas." Support your relationship by making sure you have plenty of well-being in your bank account. This tool will help you stay conscious of whether your relationship is solvent.

1. What is the status of your relationship well-being account? (check one)
   ❑ In the black
   ❑ In the red

2. Below is a chart of types of things that either add deposits or subtract withdrawals. For you, what adds or takes away the most well-being? Note which of the items listed below have a neutral, low, or high cost to your emotional well-being. For example, when one of you blames the other, is that a relatively low or high cost to the relationship bank account?

Debits	Neutral	Low (doesn't cost much)	High (big debit)
Power struggle	❑	❑	❑
Blame	❑	❑	❑
Complaints	❑	❑	❑
Being the victim	❑	❑	❑
Being the villain	❑	❑	❑
Being the hero	❑	❑	❑
Being judged or criticized	❑	❑	❑
Judging or criticizing	❑	❑	❑
Drifting	❑	❑	❑

(continued on next page)

Reactive Brain	❏	❏	❏
Being in the Triangle	❏	❏	❏
Other: _____	❏	❏	❏

Now let's look at deposits into the relationship bank account. What do you notice adds the most to your feelings of connection, flow, passion, and all-around well-being with each other?

Deposits	Neutral	Low (small deposit)	High (big deposit)
Making a great agreement	❏	❏	❏
Taking 100% responsibility	❏	❏	❏
Appreciating	❏	❏	❏
Shifting	❏	❏	❏
Creative Brain	❏	❏	❏
Playing	❏	❏	❏
Having an adventure together	❏	❏	❏
Connection	❏	❏	❏
Intimacy	❏	❏	❏
Passion	❏	❏	❏
Being loving	❏	❏	❏
Other: _____	❏	❏	❏
Other: _____	❏	❏	❏

LIVING THE BIGGEST RELATIONSHIP YOU CAN IMAGINE

part four

What would your relationship look like if
it were beyond your wildest dreams?

A Dream Come True

chapter 18

So, you're getting better at this. You can get to the bottom line of an issue clearly, speak the unarguable truth, and then move your feelings through your body. You can recognize power struggles and take steps to move out of the Triangle and back into equality and seeing your intimate others as allies.

But maybe there's still something missing. Things might have improved in your relationship, maybe tremendously, but are the big feelings back? You know, those that we feel at the beginning of relationships: the passion, the in-loveness, the great expansiveness that inspires poetry, love songs, and wonderful time spent together in bed.

The skills described thus far tend to help people move through conflict quickly and without toxicity. If you look at the relationship bank account, those skills keep the withdrawals down. An equally important skill, however, is to get really good at making new and bountiful deposits of well-being, fun, and flow so your relationship can *thrive*.

Let's start with the first move toward any manifestation: setting an intention. Take a few deep breaths, move around in your body, and imagine the kind of relationship you *really want.* Maybe you've seen it before, maybe you haven't; regardless, take the risk and make your intention as juicy and big as you can. Perhaps you don't believe that this kind of relationship is even possible. And yet, maybe it is. (Clearly, I think so.) How about taking a step out there into the great undiscovered and letting yourself want it anyway?

TOOL INTENDING THE RELATIONSHIP YOU REALLY WANT

Describe the relationship you really want.

Now make it into an intention. My intention is to have a relationship that is:

Take a few more breaths as you imagine how that kind of relationship would feel. Notice your body, and allow your feelings to come up and move through. Just keep watching, and wanting, and letting yourself feel the possibilities.

The road from intending to having is built on choosing.
Over and over and over, step by step.

Notice your new choices so far:

Old	New
Being right	Being happy
Arguing	Connecting through what is unarguable (S.E.W.)
Defending	Open, authentic, unarguable response
Righteousness	Curiosity
Blaming and complaining	Taking responsibility
Shutting down	Feeling all feelings fully; living in flow
Withdrawing	Being intimate
Emotion must be fended off or avoided	Emotion is welcomed and moved through
Drifts	Shifts
Blowing up	Timing out
Shut-down triggers	Letting triggers move through as unfelt emotion
Power leaks	Impeccable integrity
Ineffective agreements	Great and successful agreements
Parent-child	Equal co-creators
Victim, villain, hero	100% responsibility
Crappyland	Happyland

The road from intending to having is built on choosing. Over and over and over, step by step.

As you improve on the skills you're learning from this workbook, you'll notice these choices becoming increasingly available to you. And you'll realize that you can solve any conflict.

APPRECIATIONS

chapter 19

Now, let's add some rockets to your relationship, really take it to another dimension. What I'll teach you now will blast you off to a whole new world.

Have you noticed how in long-term relationships, partners can generally list all of the other's worst qualities? (I actually used to think this was my job as a "good partner," to help my partner "improve." What happened instead was that we both seemed to feel defeated and unhappy.)

While it's initially possible to hide our less-than-savory characteristics, over time we just get too tired to keep them out of sight. That's when comments like, "I finally saw who he *really* is!" tend to occur. A key to bringing passion and aliveness back to relationships that have been characterized by struggle and negativity is to refocus on what are the very best, most essential qualities about each person. That doesn't mean that the "negative" qualities are swept under the rug; rather it's about returning the focus and the balance to what we most appreciate about each other and ourselves.

The most powerful skill in this refocusing is that of giving appreciations. I first learned about appreciations from Gay and

Katie Hendricks while with them on Fiji. I was excited to go to Fiji, so didn't care what the subject matter was going to be. My heart fell, though, when I learned that we'd spend five days learning about appreciations. I figured it would take about fifteen minutes to learn everything there was. Instead, my time there opened me to the most transformative and rapid shift move I've learned. Here's how it works.

First, take a moment to make another commitment. You can either withhold or generate appreciation. Which one of these do you choose to commit to?

> I commit to withholding appreciation
> and to refusing to take in others' appreciations.
> *versus*
> I commit to being a generator of appreciation
> and to receiving others' appreciations freely.

Many of us have learned that we shouldn't hand out positive comments freely, that somehow it would give the other person "a swelled head" (quite an image, if you think about it). Taking in other people's admiration can be even more troublesome—we don't want to brag, right? What this reluctance to generate and receive does is interrupt the flow of big, expanded feelings. Like any flow of energy, creating an ongoing current of wonderful feelings depends on *all* channels being open—giving *and* receiving.

As you develop the skill of appreciation, try out the image of playing the carnival game where you hit the pad with the mallet and try to get the ball to wham up and hit the bell. Appreciating someone for what they do ("Thanks for folding the laundry," or "That was a great meal you cooked") will make the ball go up a few notches. Offering a really articulate appreciation about who someone *is* ("While you were cooking, I could see your essence awaken and could taste your loving self in every bite!") and speaking it from the heart will ring their bell. Also notice that as wonderful as it might be to receive an appreciation, being the generator can instantly expand your consciousness.

Here are some examples of some appreciations. How close do you think these would get to ringing the bell?

> "Thanks for taking the car into the shop."

> "I like the way your hair looks."

> "When I see you across the room, my heart swells."

> "As I look into your eyes, I fall in love with you all over again. I can feel your essence beaming out, your amazing loving heart, and tremendous inner beauty."

Ready to try this yourself? Look around you and find something, anything to appreciate. (Over time, I've appreciated a long list of unusual things, including tree limbs, concrete, and all manners of floor coverings.) You might find it much easier to stay in narrow focus and notice what is wrong. Appreciation requires more breadth, a wider view. It's a focus on the positive, with a sensitive awareness of previously unnoticed qualities.

TOOL   LIGHTING THE APPRECIATION FLAME

What do you appreciate right now?

What's happening in your body now?

Think about your partner. (If you don't currently have a partner, try appreciating anyone you're close to—just be sure they're not the easiest for you to appreciate.) Imagine what it is you appreciate about him or her. Take some breaths until you can really let yourself go into that space. (Sadly, I've sat with long-term partners who have had to take several minutes to think of anything at all to appreciate about each other. Like a rusted pump, your appreciation mechanism might need some oiling up.)

TOOL   APPRECIATING YOUR PARTNER

What I appreciate about my partner is:

Check in with your body sensations. What's happening now?

Here's another radical action that will enhance your life: appreciating yourself. You can do this silently or out loud. It takes care of an issue I often hear in my office: "I don't mind doing all of this for (my partner/family/job), I just wish someone would *appreciate* me for it!" I actually do this at home and feel the shift from resentment to flow. It could sound something like this: "Wow, look at what a great job I did cleaning this kitchen! Everything is sparkling!"

Here's your chance to try it out.

TOOL   APPRECIATING YOURSELF

What I appreciate about myself is:

What do you think? How do you feel?

Appreciating is a tool that can change your life. You don't have to feel it to do it; appreciation is the action that leads to gratitude. You've probably known people who are natural appreciators (you might want to appreciate them right now). Aren't they so much easier to be around than those who are complainers? Who do you want to be?

> You don't have to feel appreciative to appreciate;
> you just *choose* to appreciate.

Gay and Katie Hendricks developed the wonderfully simple and elegant exercise below. Choosing this action is a powerful step to creating a quick shift out of negativity and into expansiveness.

Giving and receiving appreciation is a habit that is well worth cultivating. I recommend a daily diet of giving and receiving appreciations, to yourself, to your loved ones, and even to total strangers.

You don't have to feel appreciative to appreciate; you just *choose* to appreciate.

TOOL   GENERATING AND RECEIVING APPRECIATIONS

(Adapted from "The Appreciation Exercise"[27] by Gay and Kathlyn Hendricks)

Take your time with this. Breathe a lot, and stay grounded in your body. If either the generator or the receiver is experiencing any glitches, slow down and be with the body sensations. Speak an unarguable truth before continuing. You can do this whole exercise by yourself, or you can have even more fun by doing this with your partner.

Generator:

What I appreciate about myself is

What I appreciate about you is

Receiver:

What you appreciate about yourself is

What you appreciate about me is

Switch roles.

MOVING BETWEEN EXPANSIVENESS AND CONTRACTION

chapter 20

Throughout this workbook I've directed you to notice your sensations. I imagine by now you've noticed that when you feel mad, sad, or scared, your body tends to close down and contract, and when you feel glad or sexual, your body opens up and expands. I think it's a splendid design that as we let ourselves fully experience emotions and flow, we tend to feel better and better.

As you become more and more tuned into your body's signals, you can actually watch yourself go up and down the ladder of expansiveness and contraction. As that happens, *notice how your beliefs about the world change accordingly.* In other words, whatever our internal experience is will dramatically impact our perception of the outside world.

Taking the steps toward shifting means fully embracing our power to create our reality.

I'll be showing you some skills that will support you being in expansiveness. As you try them out, use the scale on the next page to keep an eye on what is going on in your body. I think you'll notice that you start to feel *really* good.

Taking the steps toward shifting means fully embracing our power to create our reality.

TOOL   TRACKING YOUR CONTRACTION AND EXPANSION

Carry this tool around with you for a day or two. Set an alarm on your phone or watch to go off every hour. Make a mark at the point that most represents how contracted or expanded you're feeling at that moment. As you notice where you are on the scale, check in with your thoughts. How does your level of contraction or expansion impact what you're thinking about?

Open, expanded, loving, alive   10

Noticing contraction in different parts of body,   5
aware of different sensations moving through

Shut down, paralyzed, unable to access any   0
information about what's going on internally

TOOL   MOVING FROM CONTRACTION TO EXPANSION

In your journal, list some ways to move from contraction to expansion. (Note: Remember the Creating a Shift Repertoire tool from chapter 9? You could start with those, then add in some others that you've learned since then.)

CREATIVITY AND PLAY

chapter 21

Did you know that there is no way to *not* be creative? For those of you who think you're not creative people, take a breath. You create all the time. You might create only going to work for days on end, or create boredom, or create *Still Life Sitting on a Couch Eating Chips,* but you're creating. There's no way around it.

In relationships, we can create drama. The Karpman Drama Triangle is a tried and true method, and, in fact, is the basis for any good story. The hero saves the victim from the horrible villain (who meets some terrible fate). How many thousands of times in your life have you seen that play out? Of course you might surmise that life is only that—one long drama.

When I first learned about the Triangle, I remember feeling panicked. What would I be doing if I wasn't playing one of those roles? Wouldn't life be terribly boring?

Katie Hendricks has said that the main issue her work comes up against is with what to replace the adrenaline buzz that comes from drama.[28] People can feel high off of adrenaline. Since the fight-flight-freeze response of Reactive Brain is a very reliable way to generate adrenaline, you can see how we can become "addicted" to drama.

So what *do* we replace this power drug with? What is even better than adrenaline?

Creativity. Real creativity. Reactivity isn't creative; it's always reactive. Like having your knee tapped by the doctor, there isn't really any you in that reflex; it's just an automatic response that any reptile could have.

How does one become more creative? Many of you already have creative practices that fulfill you. Writing, visual arts, improv, dance, or athletics might fill your time. Bravo!

For those of you who are feeling scared by this whole section (a good time to breathe), just know that I felt that way, too. I mostly worked and exhausted myself (and created relationship drama) as my creative outlets. Now I have lots of things I do that fill that place in me that used to be occupied by adrenaline. The tools below will help you move in the direction of your own creativity.

Couples who did unusual activities together report more closeness and bonding than couples who fall back on their usual activities.[29]

Couples who did unusual activities together report more closeness and bonding than couples who fall back on their usual activities.

TOOL   FOLLOW YOUR IMPULSES

(Adapted from "Follow Your Impulse"[30] by Kathlyn Hendricks, PhD)

Many of us have learned to not follow our impulse. It's bad to be impulsive, right? Actually, following your impulses is the first step into your creativity, to finding the you that is under all the doing and being responsible.

Start by sitting in a chair. Sit there until you have your next impulse. It might be to scratch your nose or shift around or swallow. Wait for it . . . then just follow it. And then wait for the next one. Maybe you'll stand up or lie down on the floor. Wait . . . now follow the next impulse. Thirsty? Want to take a nap? Follow that.

You can do this for five minutes or an hour or a day. Try it out; it's one of the most delicious experiences that I have.

TOOL   FOLLOW YOUR IMPULSES TOGETHER

When I was a kid, I had my most fun hanging out with my friends and answering the question, "What do you want to do now?" We'd end up all over the place, digging holes, playing pioneer, building a clubhouse.

This tool can create that wonderful fun between you. Give yourselves a span of time (from minutes to hours to days). Keep asking the question, "What do you want to do now?" Make sure that you both are breathing and moving as you ask this, so the impulse can come from your bodies and feel in alignment. See what adventures you can co-create!

TOOL   HOW CAN WE HAVE MORE FUN?

Fun is a funny word. People have lots of ideas about what fun is supposed to look like, as if we're supposed to be the people in commercials kicking up our heels with razzmatazz grins on our faces.

While I do enjoy a good grin, fun can be all kinds of things. I view having fun as creating space to follow a creative impulse, no matter what I'm doing. That's how I end up dancing in the kitchen or racing around playing "I've Got Your Baby!" with the dogs or using a Western drawl in meetings at work. And it's how my spouse and I have bellowed out the most satisfying version of "Someone Left the Cake Out in the Rain" that I've every experienced.

Asking "How could I be having more fun right now?" adds spice to the stew of life. It connects you to your true self, the part of you that wants to express your deepest impulse right now. (In fact, how could you be having more fun reading this? Are you even comfortable in that position?) And asking, "How could we be having more fun?" opens the two of you up to adventures—and great memories—that you might never have had otherwise.

Using your journal, brainstorm ways that you might have more fun. Let your mind wander from the fast and easy (e.g., skipping on your next walk together, singing along to the radio in the car) to the more complicated (e.g., taking cooking lessons, doing an improv skit for your next social gathering).

Choosing Aliveness

chapter 22

A principle that you may have noticed as you've worked through this book is that the better you feel about you, the better you feel about other people. When you are emotionally triggered, you will project the very worst things onto those around you. When you are in ease, flow, and aliveness, suddenly everyone becomes beautiful (especially your intimate others).

You may also have noticed some familiar comfort with the old ways of feeling. Living in fear, guilt, shame, bitterness, and anger may be miserable, but most of us feel the safety of the known. Feeling loving, wonderful, and expanded can take a lot of getting used to.

One of the most important practices of all is to commit to doing those things that support you truly living in your most alive, authentic self. Let's review some of the actions that this takes:

» Speaking the truth
» Feeling all of your feelings
» Being in integrity
» Taking 100 percent responsibility for your life

» When you're drifting, committing to shifting through such activities as breathing, moving, dancing, laughing, meditating, wondering, saying something unarguable, playing.

OK, so it's time for another commitment. Use the Expansion-Contraction Scale (chapter 20) to see which commitment your body opens up to.

TOOL   CHOOSING ALIVENESS

I commit to living a life that feels familiar and predictable.

versus

I commit to choosing actions that support my full aliveness and authenticity.

Way back when, in chapter one, you made the commitment to being happy instead of being right (remember that?). That was your first step away from the familiar, what you could argue for and count on. Being happy is all about stepping off the cliff into the great unknown, the world of discovery, of potential, of possibilities. Take your partner's hand and jump off; create your own brave new world.

CHOOSING LOVE

chapter 23

Keeping connection and passion alive requires making many more deposits into the emotional bank account of a relationship than withdrawals. Appreciations, committing to shifting one's own consciousness out of contraction into expansiveness, and taking time to reconnect all are powerful additions to the resources you and your partner have to draw upon during difficult times. Creating special time together also allows for the relationship to be a rich, ongoing resource of energy and inspiration.

TOOL   CREATING CONNECTION

This exercise will help you remember what you most love about your partner. It is very helpful to do when nothing else seems to be moving you back into connection.

Stand or sit facing your partner. Place your hand on your partner's heart as you look into his eyes. Begin to breathe at the same rate. As you breathe together, look for the person that you fell in love with. (He is in there—keep looking until you find him.) Continue this for several minutes, until you feel the flow of love between your hearts, between you.

TOOL   DATES AND MYSTERY DATES

Plan at least one two-hour date per week. The definition of a date is: it is time alone for the couple, it should be fun, no difficult emotional processing will occur, and both people should show up ready to be on a date, that is, dressing up and being on their best date behavior. Alternate who is in charge of planning all the details.[31]

Mystery dates can be even more fun. The planner doesn't tell his partner what is going to happen, only what time to be ready and what to wear. (To get you started, some dates I've had with my partner include taking a picnic to the woods, zip lining, going to surprise concerts, having picnics in bed, and trying out the flying trapeze.)

TOOL   DATE PLAN

Ideas	When?	Who will plan this?

LEARNING TO LOVE YOURSELF

chapter 24

I'd like to add one last ongoing action for you to take in reliably creating expansion and movement out of contraction. That is the active choice of *loving yourself.*

Now, you've probably heard about this before. It's common knowledge that we're supposed to be able to love ourselves before we can love anyone else. But have you ever known what that really means? I didn't. I thought I had to do something good enough, be a nice enough person, achieve some amazing thing, and *then* I could love myself. What I didn't understand was that loving myself is simply a choice. An action. For no good reason except, why not?

This is another area where Gay Hendricks has lent his genius to solving a perplexing issue. His little book *Learning to Love Yourself* is full of the most concrete and helpful information about this that I've found.

Here is an exercise from that book that will dependably shift you out of contraction and into expansion.[32]

TOOL   LEARNING TO LOVE YOURSELF

(Adapted from *Learning to Love Yourself* by Gay Hendricks)

Sit in a quiet, comfortable place. Take some deep, slow breaths and begin to notice the sensations in your body.

Now think of something or someone that you love easily, thoroughly, with no obstructions. (While that could be your partner, often there are issues that get in the way of an easy loving sensation. Children, beloved pets, and places in nature can be powerful reminders of love so are a better choice when you're first trying this out.)

As you think about this person, place, or thing, notice the sensations that you feel in your body. They might include warmth, an opening in the heart area, a sense of expansion, and easier breathing.

Once you notice these sensations, see if you can breathe into them and make them even bigger. Watch them flow through your body. Play with moving them to every part of your body: up through your neck and head, down through your torso and pelvis, out through your arms and legs.

Now practice focusing this energy and playing with it. If you find any parts of your body that are tense or in pain, surround those places with this energy, as if it is bubble wrap or a blanket. Watch what happens to the contracted energy as it is surrounded by the expanded energy.

That's it! That's what loving yourself is. It is an action, a choice to create loving energy and direct it toward you. It has nothing to do with whether you deserve it or not, whether you've been good or haven't been bad. It's simply a decision to take the steps that will move you up the scale of expansion, rather than down to creating contraction. When you hear that "love conquers all," here's actual data to support that: as an energy, love has the power to shift emotional and physical density (pain, fear, sadness, tension, and anger) to emotional and physical expansiveness.

TOOL   WRITING LOVE LETTERS

Writing your partner a love letter is a wonderful way to recall the reasons you fell in love in the first place. Take your time with this and really let yourself steep in the wonderful feelings. Remember you are the source! That means you can fall in love any time, anywhere.

And if you're really daring—write a love letter to you!

epilogue

TRAVELING THE PATH TO A MAGICAL RELATIONSHIP

Relationships can seem so mysterious. Being drawn to someone, falling in love, and then the feelings somehow, inexplicably vanishing—it can all seem so out of our control. So we do the best we can. We try to "settle" in a long-term relationship, assuring ourselves that dimming down our aliveness is the price to be paid for stability. Or, if we're tired of the ongoing struggle with someone, we might decide that we just didn't choose the right person, so we end one relationship to begin another—and eventually find ourselves just as unhappy. Or we just decide to stay away from the whole mess, convinced that we're meant to be alone.

I have sat with people for hour upon hour as they desperately try to understand how to do it better, how to keep their own voice while creating deep and passionate intimacy with their partners. Throughout the early years of my own partnership, my partner and I struggled and fought and connected and experienced bliss as well as complete misery as we tried to find that exquisite balance of self and connection.

What I have gleaned from my decades of experience in the trenches (professionally and personally) is that while often complicated, relationships are not so mysterious after all. When I finally understood some elegantly simple concepts and started to apply them, I could see and experience the rewards of finding reconnection and of feeling mastery in what once seemed impossible. Time and again I observed the frustrating stuckness transforming before my very eyes into intimacy, passion, and flow.

Learning any skill takes modeling, practice, and some degree of coaching for the fine points. Now that you've made it through this entire workbook—congratulations for your commitment, by the way—you probably have tasted what I believe, with all my heart, to be the kind of magical relationship that is available to pretty much everyone. Sure, it takes some skills, some determination, and the willingness to keep trying when it seems pretty much impossible to get unstuck. All the tools I've been teaching you are logical and sequential. Even if you're clumsy when you try them, try them anyway. All of us were or are beginners at this relationship dance. If you don't worry about stepping on a few toes along the way or looking kind of goofy, you'll be pirouetting in no time.

I welcome you to the world of possibilities that your new consciousness will open up, one in which you can be authentic, be heard, and resolve conflicts quickly. I bless you as you find your own power to build the relationship of your dreams, one where you can be who you really are as you move into deep connection, aliveness, creativity, and the magic of an as-yet undiscovered world of intimacy. One where you and your beloved thrive, separately and together.

appendix 1

QUICK GUIDE TO MAKING A CHOICE

To Choose Power Struggle

» Be right (and for sure, don't be wrong)!

» Be ready to fight off other people's attempts to control you.

» Solve problems by:
  - trying to fix them by figuring them out;
  - figuring out who is to blame;
  - getting the one who is to blame to change;
  - (when that doesn't work) trying to compromise;
  - (when *that* doesn't work) fighting (wheedling, whining, collapsing, overpowering, arguing, attacking);
  - withdrawing and distancing to stop fighting;
  - enduring, knowing that this is as good as it gets.

To Choose Ease, Flow, and Happiness

» Be happy! Don't worry about being right.

» Know that you get reactive. Oh well. So does everyone else. Forgive yourself and everyone else for having Reactive Brains, and take responsibility when you react.

» Know that there are no problems to solve. Life flows when you're feeling your feelings, moving the sensations through your body, and speaking the truth. That's when you contact your full Self, your true essence.

» Remember that you're 100 percent responsible. So is everyone else. Blame is a waste of energy and gets you off track.

» Ask, how can everyone get everything they want? That's a fun, creative question.

» Remember the whole point of relationship is deep connection, passion, and aliveness. Ask, how deep can you go?

» Say to yourself, "I have no idea just how good my life can be—and I'm on the road to find out."

appendix 2

SAMPLE ANSWERS TO ARGUABLE/UNARGUABLE TRUTH EXERCISE (PAGE 18)

Arguable: You are always late.

Unarguable: I notice my stomach is tight, and I feel kind of nauseated. I feel scared. I think I'm scared about feeling out of control.

Arguable: They are really ignorant.

Unarguable: My body is contracted. As I listen to the news, I notice I feel scared. I think I'm scared about people that I don't know. Also, I feel afraid about how unpredictable life can be.

Arguable: My life sucks.

Unarguable: As I tune into my body, I notice how fatigued I feel. I also feel tightness in my shoulders and neck. I feel angry.

Arguable: I'm bad.

Unarguable: When I heard your voice, it reminded me of my mom when I thought she was mad at me. I notice my body feels collapsed. I feel sad.

Arguable: Your friends don't like me.

Unarguable: As I watched you text, I noticed that I felt a burning in my chest. I'm afraid you'd rather give your attention to your friends.

Arguable: My boss is always criticizing me. He doesn't appreciate me.

Unarguable: I'm afraid I'm not doing a good job at work.

Arguable: You don't love me.

Unarguable: I thought we were going to have sex tonight. I feel sexual. I also feel scared that you're not attracted to me anymore. I feel sad that I don't feel close to you.

Arguable: This will never work.

Unarguable: My chest feels tight and my throat has a lump in it. I feel sad about not doing what we used to do.

appendix 3

THE INNER MAP

People tend to get disoriented in the emotionally charged world of relationships. I developed the Inner Map in my own attempt to keep my wits about me. Similar to the "you are here" label that you'd find on a mall directory, I find it extremely useful to be able to locate myself according to what emotional state I'm in. Just asking myself, "where am I on the Inner Map?" can initiate my shifting out of Reactive Brain back to Creative Brain.

I added the Inner Map as an appendix in case you're interested in taking your learning to another level. While *The Relationship Skills Workbook* introduces the idea of relying on the simplicity of using only five emotions (mad, sad, scared, glad, sexual), you'll notice several other emotion labels here. These concepts actually nest together quite logically and reflect some fascinating ideas from studies about mammalian functioning as to how emotions work.

First, take a look at the inner map image on the next page and get oriented.

INNER MAP

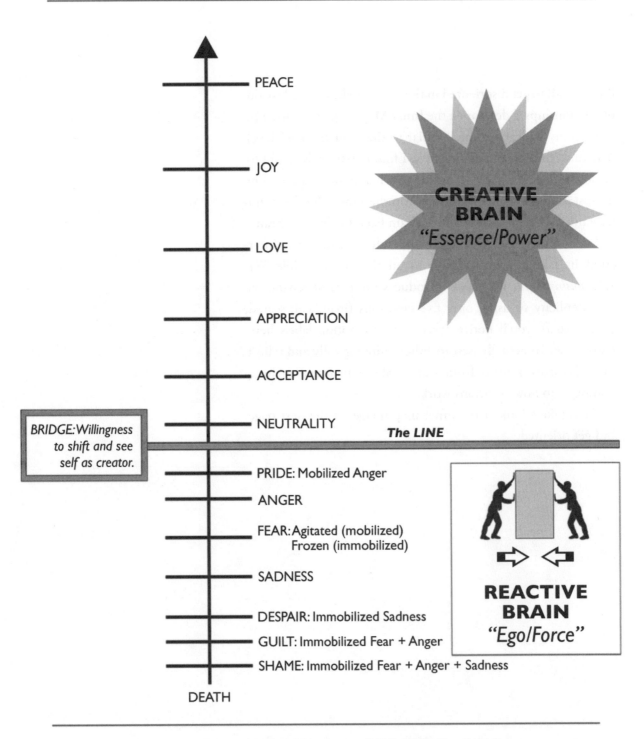

PEACE

JOY

LOVE

APPRECIATION

ACCEPTANCE

NEUTRALITY

The LINE

BRIDGE: Willingness
to shift and see
self as creator.

PRIDE: Mobilized Anger

ANGER

FEAR: Agitated (mobilized)
         Frozen (immobilized)

SADNESS

DESPAIR: Immobilized Sadness

GUILT: Immobilized Fear + Anger

SHAME: Immobilized Fear + Anger + Sadness

DEATH

CREATIVE BRAIN
"Essence/Power"

REACTIVE BRAIN
"Ego/Force"

JuliaColwell.com, based on the Map of Consciousness™ by David Hawkins, VeritasPub.com

Let me show you around.

Notice the vertical line. As you move from the bottom to the top of the line, you're moving from what has the least energy (death) to what has the most (peace). Another way to look at this is the bottom states are the most contracted, and they get progressively more expanded as you go up the line. Shame is our most contracted emotional state and is closest to death. (This is why people want to die when they feel shame.) Guilt has somewhat more energy than shame, and despair has more than guilt. People often prefer to feel anger to fear because of the burst of energy that accompanies it. And so on.

Now look at the horizontal line. This line separates Reactive Brain (or Below the Line) from Creative Brain (or Above the Line). Everything below the line is part of our automatic, immediate reactions to threat and stress. When we're Below the Line, we're reacting from threat, which puts us in the throes of our automatic patterning, also known as the "ego." Our thinking is concrete and stereotypical, our focus narrow and on what is wrong. David Hawkins (on whose Map of Consciousness the Inner Map is based) calls this the area of "Force," as our Reactive Brains tend to push and pull us into struggle and difficulty.[33]

Once we move Above the Line, our focus expands and opens. We have access to clearer thinking and problem-solving and can imagine new possibilities. Hawkins calls this zone "Power," as he views these states as being optimal for co-creativity and connection. Life flows when we're in the states Above the Line.

There are some other aspects to the inner map that I find fascinating:

> » *The inner map operates like an elevator.* It's like being in a tall department store and having the elevator door open: "Basement, Lingerie!" Whatever floor you're on is what feelings, memories, beliefs, and experiences you have access to.

» *Whatever state we're in, we believe ourselves.* Psychology calls this "state-dependent learning." The point is that once we're in a certain emotional state, we tend to remember whatever happened when we were in that state before and to not be able to access memories from other states. If we're sad, we remember other times that we felt sad and have trouble recalling feeling good. This is a self-reinforcing cycle and is often a reason people end relationships. ("I always feel this bad when I'm around you!")

» *Don't expect to feel states like neutrality, acceptance, appreciation, love, joy, and peace if you're below the line.* You can take actions that will stoke the fires of these states, but you won't feel them until you move back into Creative Brain. So don't worry if you don't feel "in love" with your partner; it's likely that you won't until you feel the expansion of being in Creative Brain.

» *Power struggle happens when we're Below the Line.* When we're Below the Line, our emotional state keeps the conflict going. Because we believe that the way we're perceiving reality is accurate, we get fixed on how *right* we are. Being in Force, that is, Below the Line, creates the entanglement of pushing the other to believe our version of reality, leading him or her to be triggered into Reactive Brain and pushing us back. If we're not conscious about what is going on, this push-pull can lead to escalation, stuckness, and relationship hell.

» *To get out of struggle, focus on moving Above the Line.* The hold that Reactive Brain has on our view of reality is the reason that *verbal processing does not help.* Our minds don't want us to believe that; our Reactive Brain minds want us to keep pushing and pulling and defending and attacking. A whole lot of energy can go into getting nowhere. Put your attention on what will help you instantly, on moving back to Creative Brain, shifting Above the Line.

» *The bridge to shifting back Above the Line is willingness.* Wanting isn't being willing. Wait until you're actually willing, then use some of the shift moves you've learned to pop yourself back up into Creative Brain.

» *Mad, scared, and sad make up all states that are Below the Line; glad and sexual are the energies behind the states Above the Line.* If you look carefully at the inner map you'll find your five old friends: mad, sad, scared, glad, and sexual.

» *In Reactive Brain, the question is: Is a person mobilized or immobilized?* Mobilization and immobilization are animal responses to threat: either we fight or flee (mobilized) or we freeze (immobilize). Look how this links up:
- Pride = mobilized anger
- Anger = anger
- Fear can separate into:
    Agitated (mobilized) fear
    Frozen (immobilized) fear
- Sadness = sadness
- Despair = immobilized sadness
- Guilt = immobilized fear + immobilized anger
- Shame = immobilized fear + immobilized anger
    + immobilized sadness

» *In Creative Brain, the question is, How good are you willing to feel?* Glad and sexual energies are the energies of Creative Brain. They are what make up the states of neutrality, acceptance, appreciation, love, joy, and peace. The difference from one state to the next is simply how expanded you are letting yourself be.

» *People in Creative Brain can solve any problem and create any new possibility.* Because people are in Power, they are co-creative, in flow, and in connection with their highest potential. This is where people feel blissful, ecstatic, and in love.

NOTES

1. For the full list of questions, see page 154 in *Conscious Loving: The Journey to Co-Commitment,* by Gay and Kathlyn Hendricks (New York: Bantam, 1992).

2. Kathlyn Hendricks, workshop communication, Santa Barbara, CA, July 2001.

3. Hendricks and Hendricks, *Conscious Loving.*

4. Temple Grandin, *Animals in Translation: Using the Mysteries of Autism to Decode Animal Behavior* (New York: Scribner, 2005).

5. Gay Hendricks, workshop communication, Banff, BC, June 2002.

6. Hendricks and Hendricks, *Conscious Loving.*

7. Kathlyn Hendricks, workshop communication, Santa Barbara, CA, September 2004.

8. Rosalind Barnett and Caryl Rivers, *Same Difference: How Gender Myths Are Hurting Our Relationships, Our Children and Our Jobs* (New York: Basic Books, 2004).

9. John Gottman, "Couples Therapy: A Research-Based Approach," *Clinicians' Video Series* (Seattle: Gottman Institute, 1997).

10. Ibid.

11. Ibid.

12. Kathlyn Hendricks, workshop communication, Santa Barbara, CA, September 2004.

13. Kathlyn Hendricks, workshop exercise, Santa Barbara, CA, February 2003.

14. Les Fehmi, *The Open Focus Brain: Harnessing the Power of Attention to Heal Mind and Body* (Boston: Trumpeter Books, 2007).

15. Gay Hendricks, workshop communication, Banff, BC, June 2002.

16. Kathlyn Hendricks, workshop exercise, Santa Barbara, CA, February 2003.

17. Gay Hendricks and Kathlyn Hendricks, *Conscious Heart: Seven Soul Choices That Create Your Relationship Destiny* (New York: Bantam, 1997).

18. John Gottman, *Why Marriages Succeed or Fail: And How You Can Make Yours Last* (New York: Simon & Schuster, 1994).

19. Gay and Kathlyn Hendricks, workshop handout, Wilsonville, Oregon, February 1995.

20. Gay and Kathlyn Hendricks, workshop communication, Savusavu, Fiji, June 2000.

21. Gay and Kathlyn Hendricks, "4 Pillars of Integrity" (unpublished).

22. Hendricks and Hendricks, *Conscious Loving.*

23. John Gottman and Nan Silver, *The Seven Principles for Making a Marriage Work* (New York: Three Rivers Press, 1999).

24. Steven Karpman, "Fairy Tales and Script Drama Analysis," *Transactional Analysis Bulletin,* (1968) 7(26): 39–43.

25. Hendricks and Hendricks, *Conscious Loving.*

26. Gay and Kathlyn Hendricks, workshop handout, Wilsonville, OR, February 1995.

27. Gay and Kathlyn Hendricks, workshop communication, Savusavu, Fiji, June 2000.

28. Kathlyn Hendricks, workshop communication, Santa Barbara, CA, July 2007.

29. Tara Parker-Pope, "Reinventing Date Night for Long-Married Couples," *New York Times,* February 12, 2008.

30. Kathlyn Hendricks, workshop exercise, Ventura, CA, March, 2005.

31. Thanks to Lin Harden for this effective strategy for creating fun together.

32. Gay Hendricks, *Learning to Love Yourself: The Steps to Self-Acceptance, the Path to Creative Fulfillment* (Ojai, CA: Hendricks Institute, 2010).

33. David Hawkins, *Power vs. Force* (Carlsbad, CA: Hay House, 2012).

RESOURCES

We are living in a wondrous time in the fields of psychology, neuropsychology, spirituality, and personal transformation. The levels of understanding of how brain functioning impacts human functioning is converging with an unprecedented ability of teachers across the planet to communicate with us.

The resources I've listed below are culled from a massive amount of information currently available about how relationships work. As I've shifted from trusting intellectualizing to trusting the authority of my own wisdom through my own body, I've become partial to teachers who teach from the body. You will find a few of those teachers in the resources below.

Books

Colwell, Julia B. *The Relationship Ride: A Usable, Unusual, Transformative Guide.* Boulder, CO: Integrity Arts Press, 2011.

I would recommend any of the many books Gay and Kathlyn Hendricks have written. Some of my favorites are:

> » *Conscious Loving: The Journey to Co-Commitment.* New York: Bantam Books, 1990.
> » *At the Speed of Life: A New Approach to Personal Change through Body-Centered Therapy.* New York: Bantam Books, 1994.
> » *Conscious Heart: Seven Soul Choices that Create Your Relationship Destiny.* New York: Bantam Books, 1997.
> » *The Big Leap: Conquer Your Big Fears and Take Life to the Next Level.* San Francisco: Harper One, 2009.

Additionally, these are some of my favorite books that have guided me along the way:

» Bekoff, Marc and Jane Goodall. *The Emotional Lives of Animals: A Leading Scientist Explores Animal Joy, Sorrow, and Empathy—and Why They Matter.* San Francisco: New World Library, 2007.

» Gottman, John. *Why Marriages Succeed or Fail: And How You Can Make Yours Last.* New York: Simon & Schuster, 1994. John Gottman's work of the past three decades on the physiology of couples in conflict has transformed the landscape of relationship work. All of his books are filled with research-oriented information; this one is a great place to start.

» Grandin, Tample. *Animals in Translation: Using the Mysteries of Autism to Decode Animal Behavior.* New York: Scribner, 2005.

» Hawkins, David. *Power vs. Force.* Carlsbad, CA: Hay House: 2012.

» Lewis, Thomas, Fari Amini, and Richard Lannon. *A General Theory of Love.* New York: First Vintage, 2000.

Tools

Here are some tools that will help you further develop your relationship abilities:

» Fehmi, Les and Jim Robbins. *The Open Focus Brain: Harnessing the Power of Attention to Heal Mind and Body.* Boston: Trumpeter Books, 2009. This clearly written book includes a CD to help you practice shifting from Narrow to Open Focus (i.e., from Reactive Brain to Creative Brain).

» HeartMath (www.HeartMath.com) has a
plethora of tools that support shifting from
reactivity to resonance (i.e., from Reactive Brain
to Creative Brain).

» Esther and Jerry Hicks (www.abraham-hicks.com)
have created many audiotapes that support the
brain to shift into an expanded state.

Videos

Simon, Tami. "Moving Beyond Blame, and Other Essential
Relationship Skills," Interview of Julie Colwell by Tami
Simon for the *Deepening Intimacy Video Series.* Boulder, CO:
Sounds True, 2014.

Gay and Kathlyn Hendricks have spent the last few years
creating a living library of their work. You can find hundreds
of videos of them on YouTube and on their website,
Hendricks.com.

ABOUT THE AUTHOR

Julia ("Julie") B. Colwell has spent over three decades and many thousands of hours with individuals, couples, and groups, exploring the world of relationships. Julie received her training as a clinical psychologist at the University of Colorado. Moving out of the world of traditional talk therapy into a body-centered focus, she's fine-tuned a style that is at once direct, respectful, gentle, confrontational, and loving, co-creating personal and relationship transformation.

Julie has a private practice in Boulder, Colorado. She is the inspiration behind and the co-founder of the Boulder Center for Conscious Community, where she teaches a range of classes, groups, and workshops, and leads the Intensive Learning Community and the Life Alignment Program.

Julie is happy to celebrate her recent marriage to her partner, Kathy, after being with her for twenty-five years. Their main vision of their relationship is to do whatever supports each of them to be happy. This vision has led them through many adventures with their beloved canine companions, friends, and chosen family.

Contact Julie at JuliaColwell.com.

ABOUT SOUNDS TRUE

Sounds True is a multimedia publisher whose mission is to inspire and support personal transformation and spiritual awakening. Founded in 1985 and located in Boulder, Colorado, we work with many of the leading spiritual teachers, thinkers, healers, and visionary artists of our time. We strive with every title to preserve the essential "living wisdom" of the author or artist. It is our goal to create products that not only provide information to a reader or listener, but that also embody the quality of a wisdom transmission.

For those seeking genuine transformation, Sounds True is your trusted partner. At SoundsTrue.com you will find a wealth of free resources to support your journey, including exclusive weekly audio interviews, free downloads, interactive learning tools, and other special savings on all our titles.

To learn more, please visit SoundsTrue.com/bonus/free_gifts or call us toll free at 800-333-9185.

SOUNDS TRUE
many voices, one journey